A KALEIDOSCOPE

SOUTH LONDON

Edited by Simon Harwin

First published in Great Britain in 1999 by
POETRY NOW YOUNG WRITERS
Remus House, Coltsfoot Drive,
Woodston,
Peterborough, PE2 9JX
Telephone (01733) 890066

All Rights Reserved

Copyright Contributors 1999

HB ISBN 0 75430 359 4
SB ISBN 0 75430 360 8

FOREWORD

This year, the Poetry Now Young Writers' Kaleidoscope competition proudly presents the best poetic contributions from over 32,000 up-and-coming writers nationwide.

Successful in continuing our aim of promoting writing and creativity in children, each regional anthology displays the inventive and original writing talents of 11-18 year old poets. Imaginative, thoughtful, often humorous, *Kaleidoscope South London* provides a captivating insight into the issues and opinions important to today's young generation.

The task of editing inevitably proved challenging, but was nevertheless enjoyable thanks to the quality of entries received. The thought, effort and hard work put into each poem impressed and inspired us all. We hope you are as pleased as we are with the final result and that you continue to enjoy *Kaleidoscope South London* for years to come.

CONTENTS

Burcu Urundul	1
Giles Wilmore	1
Ryan Millar	2
Natacha Leopold	2
R Lowe	3
Jasmeet Kalsi	4

Anerley SB School

Ashleigh Griffin	4
Scott Habgood	5
Shandale Grant	5
Michael Jones	6
Miles Bright	7
John Andrews	8

Bredinghurst School

John Peterson	8
Raphael McLellan	9
Karl Barrett	10

Chestnut Grove School

Erif Petch	11
Jamie West	12
Leon G Jones	12
Tyrone Murray	13
Mitchell Priest	14
Yasar Ozbaris	14
Henry Yanney	15

Graveney School

Tim Malcolm	15
Kaylisha Archer	16
Chris Malcolm	17

Damien Shannon	18
Charlotte Atkins	19
Gabriel Byng	20
Chris Marsh	20
Sam Whannel	21
Amna Mirza	22
Shak Yousaf	22
Oliver Ovenden	23
Nithya Jeganathan	24
Kasia Brookes	24
Katy Oglethorpe	25
Rosemary Pycock	26
Pia Sanchez	26
Emily Xiao Mei	27
Sophie Langridge	28
Michelle Da Silva	29
Emma Kelly-Hollin	30
Nicholas Barker	31
Danielle Plummer	32

Grey Coat Hospital School

Holly Wilson	32
Tasha Sinclair	33
Tamika Roper	34
Faye Paget	35

James Allen's Girls' School

Kathryn Marle	35
Jenny Lau	36
Sanchia Purkayastha	36
Samantha German	37
Natasha Nixon	38
Natasha Vowles	38
Nina McDermott	39
Leili Farzaneh	40

Divya Pande	40
Sophie Gilbert	41
Victoria Trevelyan	41
Paola Rodriguez	42
Charlie Parker	42
Stephanie Bartscht	43
Natalie Barry	44
Sarah Godden	45
Dorothy Joe	46
Elizabeth Cook	46
Karen Amoa	47
Catriona Lucas	47
Sheila Jen	48
Bridget Whelan	48
Claudia Kemp	49
Chenat Madziwa	49
Inessa Samokhvalova Goodman	50
Stephanie Williams	50
Amelia Scott	51
Sheena Patel	51
Leonie Stone	52
Purni Patel	53
Aletia Aston	53
Alice Mackay	54
Jasmine Patel	54
Maria-Louisa Norris	55
Tanya Lake	55
Olivia Stredder	56
Julia Nawrocki	57
Sarah Castor-Perry	57
Jessica-Ann Jenner	58
Chloe Hayward	59
Polly Davidson	59
Josephine Pell	60
Efua Mercer	60

Laura Whitehead	61
Temitope Popoola	62
Elizabeth Lim	63
Rosie Simmons	64
Hannah Battershell	64
Sasha Milavic Davies	65
Marina Harnik	66
Georgina Warren	66
Caitlin Albery Beavan	67
Christine Szekely	67
Rosalind Tew	68
Sandra Djokic	68
Katie Prescott	69
Amna Ahmad	70
Eliza Ward	70
Sahra Janmohamed	71
Jessie Smart	72
Laura McCahery	73
Rebecca Clarke	73
Zoë Abrahams	74
Florence McHugh	75
Kate Rodney	76
Gemma Ford	76
Megan Fisher	77
Ellie Davies	78
Jackie Steward	78
Nicola Garland	79
Lucy Anne Hutchinson	80
Abigail Zeitlin	81
Amy Fitzpatrick	82
Megan Warwick	82
Celeste Tobias-Freitag	83
Polly Southern	84
Helen Wade	84
Natalie Yakimiuk	85

Milly Jarvis	85
Letitia Barry	86
Rachel Russell	86
Lucy Merrell	87
Laura Cooper	88
Melissa Lawrence	89
Lily Arnold	89
Alex Parsons	90
Alex Cairns	90
Keshvi Prajapati	91
Natasha Almuli	92
Alex Mathias	92
Yasmin Hasan	93
Sarah Enderby	94
Clare Cheeseman	95
Magdalena Powell	96
Sophie White	96
Matilda Radcliffe	97
Eleanor Harris	97
Gemma Gaitskell-Phillips	98
Nina Wafula	98
Lucy Taylor	99
Shreya Raghuvanshi	100
Jessica Clark	100
Nneoma Ulu	101
Stefanie Menashe	102
Emma Findlay	102
Claire Willman	103
Katie Harney	103
Nadia Elsadani	104
Omolola Akitoye	104
Federica Amati	105
Eleanor Simon	105
Francesca Sidhu	106
Shalini Anand	106

Kate Macrae	107
Alice Philipson	108
Natasha Evans	108
Rosalind Pedder	109
Emily Ashworth	109
Stephanie Burton	110
Sophie Willmington	111
Chloe Palmer	111
Chioma Onwubalili	112
Beatrice Smith	112
Alice Michell	113
Alex Wigley	114
Camellia Makhzoumi	114
Laura Hooper	115
Alanna Barber	116
Isabel Jarrett	116
Laura Tucker	117
Katsura Leslie	118
Francesca Tyler	118
Lia Deraniyagala	119
Camilla Spoto	120
Kate Stevinson	121
Shaista Mufti	122
Nicola Roden	122
Laura Parrish	123
Neusha Milanian	124
Victoria Rolfe	124
Veronique Watt	125
Cassie Robertson	126
Kate Fletcher	127
Denise Li	128
Nadia Huq	128
Susan Mulanda Dale	129
Ali Paget	130
Natasha Rodionova	131

Stephanie Davies	132
Niamh Riordan	132
Laura Myers	133
Shakia Stewart	134
Penny Walsh	134
Suhanya Balasingham	135
Saba Khan	136
Suha Shariff	136
Louise Dalton	137
Sarah Harper	138
Emily Willson	139
Amy Wynne-Jones	140
Susan El-Ghoraiby	140
Phillipa Brothwood	141
Lizzie Sells	142
Victoria Mercey	142
Tara Brown	143
Jessica Bland	143
Sophie Stanhope	144
Christina Stoneman	144
Chloé Beecham	145
Claudia Moselhi	146

Kidbrooke School

Emma Cleary	147
Vimala Ramalingum	147
Thuan Ho	148
Sumith Suri	148
Arti Hirani	149
Joanne Oringa	149
Saulo R Moreira	150
Laura Cullen	150
Faye Dar	151
Indika Malleuwe	151
Ryan Hayes	152
Kira Etherington	152

Satwant Bansal	153
Adam Fuller	153
Kerry Vincent	154
Lee Nicholls	154
Simon Foley	154
Adelaide Mendy	155
Sarah-Jane Bailey	156
Lisa San	156
Anne Louch	157
Angela Pearson	157
Nathaniel Gray	157
Matthew Baiden-Adams	158
Tamla Jane Hall	158
Vinh San	159
Jenna Seymour	159
Reece Parkinson	160
Chrissy Sheridan	160
Claire Reader	161

Prendergast School

Rachel Dunk	161
Tara Smyth	162
Simone Peynado Clarke	162
Claire Carbin	163
Louise Smith	164
Natisha Salih	164
Adele Scott	165
Charlotte Macrae	166
Natreema Kusi-Mensah	167
Karin Diamond	168
Aysen Estref	168
Natasha Coleman	169
Nneka Carr	170

Putney Park School
- Sophie Bigmore — 170
- Lucia Sabine — 171
- Elizabeth Carter — 171
- Sarah Wheatley — 172
- Penny Harland — 172
- Elizabeth Straughan — 173
- Hannah Nurse — 173
- Emma Hazou — 174
- Poppy Willcox — 175
- Rana Haddad — 176
- Elizabeth Shone — 176
- Nina Thomas — 177
- Chloé Bellas — 178
- Lindsay Garland — 178
- Nicola Vasey — 179
- Camilla Hayes — 180

Riverston School
- Emma Chapman — 181
- Sunil Sonny — 182
- Richard Bond — 182
- Wing-Ho Tang — 183
- Rian Butler — 183
- Wai Kit Lam — 184
- Benjamin Wilkinson — 184
- Monique Grant — 185
- Samed Aykac — 185
- Olufemi Okulaja — 186
- Rebecca Penfold — 186
- Maryanne Carlin — 187
- Niyi Falase — 187
- Daniel Olurin — 188
- Lena Andreou — 189
- Hurshal Patel — 189

Pinkesh Patel	190
Gemelle Canoville	190
Nick Philp	191
Michael John	191
Lianne Hemblade	192
Shaheen Ali	192
Nicola Watson	193
Rolande Seudieu	193
Chris Bancroft	194
Michael Ehinmoro	194
Scott Simpson	195
Bilal Elahi	195
Gavin Burton	196
Rochelle Edmondson	196
Leon Powell	197
Charantoor Singh	198
James Martin	198
Esther Harrison	199
Tunde Dele-Ademola	200
Stacey Bogle	201
James Allen-Thompson	201
Claire Pink	202
Lanre Falase	203
Natasha Clarke	203
Katie Firmin	204

St Saviour's and St Olave's School

Tolu Ogundipe	204
Rebecca Reed	205
Ali Cairns	205
Omotola Awofidipe	206
Kelly Fordree	207
Seyi Omotayo	207
Folu Akintola	208
Judy Antwi-Ohenewah	208

Shamama Abulkhairi	209
Claire Hillaby	210
Carmen Gowie	211
Bianca Jacobs	212
SalinaTon	213
Krystal Stewart	214
Chloe Trezel	214
Mumtaz Sadique	215
Farishta Karwani	215
Juliana Mensah	216
Sunna Komal Pervaiz	217
Sharon Oteng	218
Cherish Akinleye	219
Anna Friewald	220
Laura Johnson	221
Natalie Jerrom	221
Filiz Altinoluk	222
Victoria Hayden	223
Sufia Khatun	223
Jackie Lai	224

Streatham High School
Leyla Guler	225

Ursuline High School
Olivia Firmin	225
Natalie Isaia	226
Sian Wilson	226
Holly Hawthorn	227
Saba Hayat	228
Hayley King	228
Athena Stavrakis	229
Quetzal Rivas	229
Niyla Javaid	230
Rochelle Sheldrick	230

Jenny Davies	231
Imogen Barraclough	232
Cristna Araujo	232
Claudia Brady	233
Natalie Solgala-Kaz	234
Rachel Shepherd	234
Gail Clark	235
Nicola Burden	236
Rebecca O'Connor	236
Tanya Mehmet	237
Katie Jodoin	238
Monica Carvalho	238
Ella Horswell	239
Catriona Maria McCarthy	240
Darya Syrpis	240
Virginia Stonehill	241
Pedrina Rodrigues	242
Kayenaat Gova	242
Medena Knespl	243
Delisa Ribaudo	243
Helen Onafowokan	244
Alice Marcar	244
Maria Garbutt-Lucero	245
Nicole Charles	246
Reem Nasser	246
Joanna Foster	247
Karen Dempster	247
Charlene Cumming	248
Maria Kadziola	248
Liezl Ann Ornzo	249
Izabela Stacewicz	249
Laura Attipoe	250
Charlotte Sewell	251
Amy Allen	252
Emma Bye	253

Dahye Chung	253
Lehanna Young	254
Antoinette Bynoe	254
Marianne Gray	255
Natasha Gordon	255
Laura Bye	256

The Poems

I Think I Am In Love

I think I am in love,
with a guy I've known for centuries.
He is real cute,
plus he is also cool.
He is a boy,
as always with his boyish faults,
but he seems to be trying
just to make me smile,
rather than ending up in
another row.
He can be careless,
but he is a laugh,
after all, without boys
there would be no more
fun on the beach,
but without boys, perhaps there
would be no more wars over the beach!
But he is a boy and this time I really do think
that I am in love with him.

Burcu Urundul (16)

Journey For Nothing

Down the street, across the lake,
around the corner, past the snake
in the zoo,
nip to the loo,
across the bridge, through the gate,
better go, quick it's 10 to 8.
Cross the road, up the hill,
time to rest, we've got time still.
Finally get there, just in time,
all this journey for a poem that rhymes.

Giles Wilmore (11)

SARAH

I remember it like it was yesterday.
You and I would go walking along the beach in the sunset hand in hand.
We would stare at the sea, glistening in the dying sun.
You said that one day you and I would travel across that deep blue something called the sea.

It never happened.
We never did go on that journey.
The night you left, I was late because I had gone to get the tickets.
I came home, you were gone.
No letter, no note.
Just the sweet smell of your perfume.

You never came home.
All that night I tossed and turned like a lion battling a wildebeest.
There were just too many questions that needed answering.
The house is still lonely.
There's no brilliant sapphire eyes or rose-red lips to wake to.

Please, Sarah, come back.

Ryan Millar (12)

PEACE

Peace is freedom
Peace is stardom
Peace is unity
Peace is equality
Peace is a life without violence
Peace is confidence
Peace is what you inherit
Peace is a spirit
Peace is above all, *love!*

Natacha Leopold (14)

A Cold, Dark Night

I sit here alone watching the raging fire flames
warming my bones,
with a glass of whisky in a dimly lit room.
I gaze towards the window, snow falls heavily.
Outside, snow is pressing against the window ledges.
In the corner, my Christmas tree stands
lightly decorated, underneath lays one small gift.
As I look on I see the milk and mince pies I've left
for my very special visitor.
The smells coming from the small kitchenette are of
turkey roasting in the oven with chestnut and apple
stuffing, small cocktail sausages rolled in bacon,
Christmas pudding steaming with holy around,
mistletoe hanging over the door.
The drinks stand so proud on the side, advocaat, whisky,
brandy and port just a small blend I thought.
The table is set but only for one, and in the middle
I've placed the grand Christmas cake that with preparation
took a whole month to make.
Setting the fruit punch from Granny's old recipe.
What a brilliant occasion this will be, carol singers on
Christmas Eve will make it even more special for me.

R Lowe (14)

THE WAY THINGS USED TO BE

No matter what I say or do,
I'm still gonna feel hurt,
I can't bottle up how I feel,
That just makes it worse.

I wake up and feel sad,
I think about him and go mad,
But now I know it's over,
Time will help me recover.

I never knew it would be so hard,
To live through guilt and pain,
I never want to go through this,
Ever again.

I thought it was love, he thought it was lust,
He took advantage of me and my trust,
Still to this day,
The heartbreak drives me mad,
'Cause I look back and remember what I had.

Jasmeet Kalsi (15)

ASHLEIGH

A stonishing
S mart
H andsome
L ikeable
E xtra
I ntelligent
G reat
H appy.

Asheligh Griffin (12)
Anerley SB School

SKY POEM

I fly in the clouds so high up above
the blue and white sky.

I see people walking
I see people talking
I see people fighting
I see people working.

I start to look for somewhere
to land and have my lunch,
a nice cheese sandwich.
Nothing else to eat but
that cheese that makes me fly
so high up in the sky.

Scott Habgood (12)
Anerley SB School

SCIENCE IS . . .

Science is
stupendous.
It's satisfactory
and significant.
In science,
we have a sequence
of signs,
some smells
and a few
satellites,
but it's safe.

Shandale Grant (12)
Anerley SB School

THE BEST INVENTION IN THE WORLD

If I invented a machine for myself
It would make all my dreams come true
It would bring me a house as big as a palace
I would decorate it with statues and pictures of animals
I would have a pool in the garden as big as a classroom
And a Jacuzzi full of bubbles with champagne on the side

My invention would build me a car
A limousine of the whitest white
To ride around with all my friends
It could turn into a Ferrari
At the flick of a switch
You could fold it into a suitcase to save on parking

Next my machine would build me a shopping centre
So I could do my shopping without having to go out
There would be al the best things to eat and drink
Like MacDonald's, Kentucky, BK and pizza
If I got too fat my machine would help me lose weight

My machine would make things for everyone I love
A present for my baby sister
More for my sisters and brothers
A chain with a ring for mum and dad
Sports gear for all my mates

I will build my invention in my dreams at night.

Michael Jones (14)
Anerley SB School

UNDER THE SEA

I go deep
I go deep under the sea
and I want to see
I want to see everything
under the sea
under the sea

I feel free
deep, deep
under the sea.

I feel so cool
in the sea
just like I want to be.

Under the sea,
where it's free,
and there's just me.

Miles Bright (12)
Anerley SB School

METALS

Aluminium as light as a feather
Antimony is hard and brittle
Arsenic, don't eat it or you'll be dead
Barium, you would not like a meal of this either
Chromium makes your bike look cool
Zinc for a coat will stop you from rusting
Lead is heavy and poisons fish
Platinum much rarer than gold
Gold makes people go crazy with greed
Silver is the money in your pocket
Steel keeps our factories up and running
Iron will turn red in the rain.

John Andrews (14)
Anerley SB School

WHAT WAS THAT?

Bump!
What was that?
Just me, the flea
Bong!
What was that?
Just John, singing a song.
Kapow!
Ow,
What was that?
Just Patty, giving Landy a slappy.
Ding Dong!
What was that?
That's the end of the poem, son.

John Peterson (14)
Bredinghurst School

True Soul Meaning

I walk alone
a free spirit.
All of the different faces
I see,
leering, pointing, whispering.
They follow me
with wandering eyes,
suspicious, nervous, cautious.
They've heard about me,
about what I'm supposed to have done.
They don't understand,
they don't know,
the way they react,
so out of proportion.
No trust,
no faith.
Everywhere I go
I'm cast disparaging looks,
I'm tired of it,
just damn tired of it.
That's cool though,
I can handle it!

Raphael McLellan (15)
Bredinghurst School

KARL'S POEM

Am going insane,
Inside ma brain,
It's so much pain.

Sometimes I can't even concentrate, too much voice.
Ma brain can't even co-ordinate, but it's their noise.
I can't take it anymore, kicking the door,
Throwing each other on the floor.

Am going insane,
Inside ma brain,
It's so much pain.

Why don't the kids just sit on their chair?
You probably don't care.
But you need your education
So you can work at your occupation.
You might even become famous
And surprise the whole nation.

Am going insane,
Inside ma brain,
It's so much pain.

But you gotta see what you wanna be and don't flee.
Failing in your exams hurts like a wounded knee.
Just be cool and go to school and even pray all day.
So God can bless and when you ask for a job
The manager can say yes and make success.
If you wanna be it, you gotta do it, the sky's the limit.
You gotta get a grip before you flip.
Don't want to crack upon the kerb and then trip.

Am going insane,
Inside my brain,
It's so much pain.

Karl Barrett (14)
Bredinghurst School

THE WORLD'S ASLEEP

As the sun goes down for the night
And the moon comes into sight
The world's asleep
No one to weep
No one to laugh
No one to cry
No one to gaze at the midnight sky.

The troubles and trials are over
The day has seen its last
The world's asleep
The world's asleep
Goodnight
Choi
Au revoir.

Erif Petch (12)
Chestnut Grove School

SIN

The cold, dark night
Crawling down your back
Stirring the fright
Is the night so black

You look around
You see a shack
You've reached the point
Of no turning back

A mind and a face
To haunt the eye
Gone without a trace
You wave goodbye

Like an old fairytale
You walk straight in
You know you have failed
You're as shameful as sin.

Jamie West (12)
Chestnut Grove School

AT NIGHT I DREAM OF BEING AN ARTIST

At night I dream of being an artist,
I dream that all night long
Big, bright pictures from my comics
Impress upon my mind.
Ideas keep on flowing like the sea,
Colours clashing, colours flashing
Into my mind.
I see the paints, dark and light,
As bright as the moon in the dark, black night.

At night I dream of being an artist,
Creating different styles of drawing.
I see the statues standing high,
Wide as the ocean, tall as the sky.
I see myself making models day by day,
Never giving up with the soft clay.
I see my creations come to life,
And play my games all through the night.

Leon G Jones (14)
Chestnut Grove School

SUMMER

It's hot
It's fun
You go out places

You party
You dance
You're in shorts and T-shirt

You run
You jog
You're exercising

It's wicked
It's great
It's *summer.*

Tyrone Murray (13)
Chestnut Grove School

MOTHER

Once I had a dear old mother, who was very kind to me,
When I got into trouble, she sat me on her knee.

One night as I was sleeping, upon my feather bed,
An angel came from heaven, and told me Mum was dead.

So I woke up the next morning, to see if it was true,
Yes, Mum had gone to heaven, up in the sky so blue.

So, children obey your parents, and do as you are told,
'Cause if you lose a mother, you lose a heart of *gold!*

Mitchell Priest (13)
Chestnut Grove School

AS WHITE AS SNOW

Snow, snow, oh what a glory,
Snow, snow, all over the morning,
White, crisp, fresh virgin snow,
Snow, snow, as white as sheep,
Snow, snow, soft like sleep,
Snow, snow makes you feel happy inside,
When you see it settle outside,
Peaceful, innocent snow,
Snow, snow, oh what a feeling.

Yasar Ozbaris (13)
Chestnut Grove School

Arsenal Poem

Arsenal are the greatest team,
With players no one has ever seen.
Bergkamp, Anelka ready to score,
Chistopher Wreh gonna bag four.
Champions League is a big step up,
Higher than FA and Worthington Cup.
Thanks to players like Vieira and Petit,
Arsenal will hardly see a defeat.
As long as Arsenal are here to stay,
Watch out United, we're on our way.

Henry Yanney (12)
Chestnut Grove School

Death Of Innocence

I wait, heart in mouth, sweating with the cold touch of fear.
Images fluttering through my mind, the tension is too great.
The imminent crash, the piercing screech, awaited by my baited ears.
Shining metal glances in the sun,
The hum of the motor,
The slow grinding of the machine
Rushes past me, leaves blowing in its wake.
The patter of tiny feet emerges on the gleaming tarmac,
The innocence of life stands, oblivious to danger.
My eyes cloud over as the piercing screech cuts through my body,
I run, adrenaline throbbing through me.
I stumble to the ground, panting breath, my head aches as blood
Rushes to my head, I rub my eyes yet all I see is blood,
The still, lifeless form lies there, burned into my memory.
I ask myself, why?
Why must life end in such violent forms.
When death itself is punishment enough?

Tim Malcolm (15)
Graveney School

LAVERNE IS HER NAME

She makes everyone feel like the flea-bitten cat next door,
When people walk past her they cringe,
She has a high-pitched voice with sounds like a car skidding down the road,
Her sense of dress has gone,
The bright pink shorts don't match with the grey moth-bitten jacket,
The teachers think she is a saint but she's worse than being strapped to a chair watching 'Noddy'!
Her so-called friends are revolted by her but they can't tell her that or she'll knock them to blocks,
The hair on her head sticks up on end like wheat growing in the summer sun,
Her eyes are beady and scheming,
Her lips are dry and caked up with Vaseline,
The odour she gives out is vile and it smells like chicken sick that's ten days' old,
She makes pupils and teachers nervous,
Bully is what you call her,
She threatens, torments, harasses, terrorises and intimidates everyone in her path,
She's the controller of your nightmare,
The person you've always dreaded,
Even though I feel this way about her,
I still have to see her tomorrow,
Laverne is her name so beware.

Kaylisha Archer (11)
Graveney School

MRS BRINKLY

The dreaded dinner lady
Stands there
Looking with her big, grey eyes,
Standing straight like an army sergeant.
If you make one wrong move, you're dead.
Silence as she walks down the corridor,
If you talk you're done for.
I get into a fight,
She sees me,
Now I'm in for it.
I start running and running,
She shouts,
The whole playground freezes over,
Nobody moves.
The only sound is the slow pounding of my heart,
She calls, 'Christopher'
The whole playground turn their heads
And looks at me.
I can feel my face burning up,
I slowly walk up to her,
She slowly agonisingly says,
'Against the wall Christopher.'

Chris Malcolm (11)
Graveney School

SATURDAY AT THE FOOTBALL

It is hard to explain the kind of passions
that run loose on a Saturday afternoon
down at the football ground.
The pre-match atmosphere, the cheers
as the players run out onto the neat grass.
The cheers of the fans to
the home team and the jeers at the visitors
are common place.

Anyone who goes to football matches will
say that there are many emotions
running through the ground,
Exhilaration and desperation as the score changes.
The common cries of 'Handball,' 'Foul,'
'Are you blind ref' can be heard
at every match. I never let my
emotions out quite like I do at the footy.

'One-nil,' 'Penalty,' 'Goal,' all these
words will hold a special place in
my heart. There really is nothing like
Saturday at the football.

Damien Shannon (15)
Graveney School

GRANDAD

I was only young when it happened,
Too little to know what it meant.
I finished my school day as usual,
And waited for Mum at the gate.

But today was somewhat different,
For instead of my mum - stood my aunt.
And there inside of the bright yellow car,
My uncle sat patiently waiting.

'Mum's not feeling too well' Uncle said,
As I clambered into the car.
The journey was deathly silent,
But I was only young - I didn't care.

When I got home Mum was waiting,
And Dad and some relatives too.
Their painted smiles and bleary eyes,
Just greeted me one by one.

The living room showed signs of a party,
Disappointment spread through my body,
And the tears pricked my eyes,
'Why did you have a party when I had to go to school?'

Mum and Dad nodded at each other,
Then Dad led me up the stairs.
He held my hands tightly then told me,
That Grandad would no longer be there.

The room was filled with bright, coloured flowers,
Each one saying 'Dad' or 'Grandad'.
It was only then that I realised,
My grandad was forever gone.

Charlotte Atkins (15)
Graveney School

HIM

His shop is just like all the others,
No one ever seems to be in there,
Maybe a few seedy characters clutching top-shelf mags.
It's just him though, all grimy fingers and long fingernails.
He has got a respectable face with a sort of down-town vulnerability,
A very straight back
His main occupation is watching the small telly that nestles in
                                                          the corner.
He is always in there - never a wife like the ones down Brixton Hill.
He never talks but not in a surly way.
He looks religious, sort of holy.
Slightly superior though not trying to be patronising,
Well, he couldn't not in that grimy shop.
He always wears an occupied expression,
Never in a mood.
He always seems so stable.
After all he is just a News Agent . . .

Gabriel Byng (11)
Graveney School

IN THE DARK

In the darkness,
Shadows chase each other in the corner of my eye,
A demon stands silhouetted against my curtains,
Where my coat should be hung.
He stands silently,
And watches me.
The creaking of an old house,
Or clawed feet padding softly on carpeted floor.
Underneath my bed,
Yellow eyes glow with anger,
As the silent shrieks of the night creatures fill the air,
A clammy hand feels its way towards me.

In the darkness they surround my despairing soul,
Drawing closer and closer with every flicker of my eye,
I lie wide awake in that eternal night.
I dare not sleep for they will come.

Chris Marsh (15)
Graveney School

INJURY TIME

We walked down the path as one
Looking forward to the day ahead
Breezes flew through my hair

We laughed and joked so unaware
But as we drew closer tension mounted
For we were nearly there

The tarmacked road stared back at us
We grew afraid of what was to come
Still cross that road we must

Memories are strange and tangled
Some disappear with age
Lost in a mess of chemicals inside your head
But, some day, vivid and alive

The word 'No' echoes in my head
Ignored, I see a flash of images
A picture, etched onto my brain
Of flaying arms and legs
On a silver body.

Sam Whannel (15)
Graveney School

TRUST

She walked down ahead of me
She turned, the other way that I had thought it would be.
Confused. I followed keeping in step
Though talking, questioning, trying to fill the gap
Which lay between my mother and me.
I never thought that this is how it would be
When my mother found out. But then
How can I explain when she promised never to listen again
To what I had to say. So I
Decided never again to lie
To her again. Though what was I to do when she
Walked right past, ignoring me.
I remembered the days we would sit and just talk
About nothing in particular or maybe take a walk
In the garden. She would then stop and notice a fair
Flower, pick it then tie it in my hair.
I know that I can never turn back time
So I pray that some day she will forgive my crime.
I never realised how much damage I had done
Our precious relationship had just . . . gone.

Amna Mirza (15)
Graveney School

THE OCEAN AND ITS PEACE OF LIFE

Supposedly they're the role models
So growing up with a short temper and a loud mouth,
Was what *I* learnt from *H*im.

Whether growing up like that was,
A good or a bad thing,
I just knew that,
This figure's footsteps were the ones *I* had to follow.

*H*e argued with *H*er,
And *S*he argued with *H*im.
Then *H*e left and *S*he was given the gift of life,
And suddenly, the ocean washed away the battleground,
And all fell silent.

Although nine years may have passed,
I do find myself following *H*is footsteps,
As now,
I see myself arguing with *H*er,
And *H*er arguing with *M*e.

Shak Yousaf (16)
Graveney School

MOVING

Moving for me
Never contained the modern pressures
The stress, the strain, lost keys and tearful departures
For me always a time of adventure
Of change, of stories, of laughter
There were new rooms to search, new halls to run
Within shaking cabins I could watch
Plastic bags of life's treasures making the journey
Scurrying here, scampering there, often a nuisance
But always looked after

With packed brown boxes
Large moving clocks
Stuck sofas and beds that were broken
Giant smoking lorries and houses with mouses
How come always on the top floor?

Oliver Ovenden (15)
Graveney School

GRANDMOTHER

I have always admired her,
Even though she is not with me now,
I feel her in my blood,
Most people say grandmothers are cranky,
But not this one

I feel her speak to me,
She has a soft gentle voice,
Soft as the wind blowing,
I feel I can only talk to her,
My parents are busy,
My brother goes to university.

When she died I cried,
But I knew that people had to die one day,
It was like a chapter in a book,
I had to get on with my life,
And put the past behind me,
But I will always miss her.

Nithya Jeganathan (11)
Graveney School

TRANSCENDENCE

There was a drunken party on the shore, when I stepped out,
Into icy raven water, to escape their drunken shouts.
But the music became distant and the coldness ebbed away,
As we swam over sleeping fish and out beyond the bay.

The huge full moon cast shadows on our faces and the sea,
Our eyes grew wide and blacker and we swam on breathlessly,
And the figures on the each yelled out, afraid that we had sunk,
That night, I think it's them that drowned in everything they'd drunk.

But we lay back in melted moon, and gazed up into glass,
Majestically, encrusted thick, with millions of stars.
To the end of the world and off the edge, into infinity,
Enveloped in that liquid sky - black, celestial sea.

There were some passed-out people on the shore, when we returned.
A heap of smoking ashes where the bonfire had burned.
Piles of vodka bottles lying empty on the sand.
The night that we swam out to sea,
And I never came back to land.

Kasia Brookes (16)
Graveney School

TRUE HATE

Sitting in the gutter, thoughts running through my head,
What have I done to offend her, what on earth have I said?
Tears falling from my swimming eyes, of anger and of hate.
I *could* tell an adult, but I know it's now too late.
My wounds continue throbbing; 'I fell off the bus again.'
I grit my teeth as I suffer from the never-ending pain.
What *is* wrong with me, my religion or my face?
Or is it my height, or possibly my race.

Why can't she stop haunting me?
And just for once let it be.
I can see a car approaching, I mustn't be late,
To test my miserable life in the hands of fate.

Katy Oglethorpe (11)
Graveney School

WINDOW INTO MY SOUL

Within a place called Dreamworld there lies a blue, blue sea,
And in that blue sea of mine there sits the window into my soul.
My soul is filled with different things.
Different feelings, different memories and different emotions.
My soul is a place where I can sit and dream up all my dreams.
I dream up places, lands and worlds, different thoughts and tunes.
The tunes are heavenly, colourful and bright.
In my heart there is my sky filled with stars, moons and suns.
In my sky are my dreams.
In my dreams are my feelings.
In my feelings sits my blue, blue sea,
And in my blue, blue sea stands the window into my soul.

Rosemary Pycock (11)
Graveney School

ISMAIL

There was something strange about Mum,
Her hand always placed on her tum.
Short hair now growing in bursts,
The need to quench her great thirst.
The fact that her waist had increased,
The reason she could get no sleep.
The answer to why she would sit,
In the front room and constantly knit.
The response to anything was to cry,
Or at other times she would just sigh.
I never thought to question my mother,
I knew that there was to be another.

Pia Sanchez (15)
Graveney School

OLD TIME, SWEET TIME

New term came again,
Standing in the centre of the playground,
I was wandering around.
I felt loneliness and everything seemed so silent.
Only the wind was striking my face.
The old times occurred to me.

Reading stories with year three;
Doing poem audition;
Playing games with classmates;
Going on exciting school trips;
Have the girls' secret talking . . .

And friends!
Oh, that's the worst, I missed a lot of them.
We had a nice teacher too,
Just like my mum sometimes,
Primary school is really lovely, unforgettable . . .

My heart beating fast with sadness, I know I was going to cry.
But facing a new secondary school,
I stopped this feeling because I know this is a new start for me.
And I hope it'l be as memorable as ever.

Emily Xiao Mei (11)
Graveney School

TIME SANDS

There was a big wall at the bottom of our garden,
it towered up and up and up, right into the sky.
I was told that the giants lived over it,
but no matter what I did,
how high I climbed,
how much I longed to see,
I could not look over that wall.
It was strong,
like a fort,
covered in ivy that crackled,
but without a single slit to peep through.
Sounds of laughter and scuffles,
whispers,
secrets
echoed around the garden's still, fresh, greenness.
But I didn't care for the garden,
I had climbed that wall.
It didn't matter how sweetly the birds sung,
or how the flowers burst through,
showering sweet scented fairy dust over the lawn,
or that the grass waved and beckoned to me,
tickling my bare feet.
I cared only for the big world over the wall,
the world I could not be a part of.
But now, here I stand on the cold, harsh concrete of that world,
I look at the wall,
much smaller now,
and once again I wish to be over it.

Sophie Langridge (15)
Graveney School

WE WAIT AND WONDER

Pacing, waiting, whispering,
Darkness descends again
The air is motionless, stifling
As we wait and wonder.
Echoes along the corridor,
Sickly, sour smell
A door creaks slowly open
A distant voice speaks:
'You can come in now.'
There he lies, frail and feeble
Tired of life's endless battles,
Limp, wasted body spread out on crisp, white sheets,
Pale face gaunt and tormented.
Our hearts are lumps of lead,
Liquid crystal pours from eyes like a river
Undammed,
Steady bleeps pierce my thoughts.
Time suddenly stops.
Steady beeps become one long note, shrill and
Penetrating.
Rushing, trying, crying
The battle is over.

Michelle Da Silva (15)
Graveney School

MISS X

I sit down in assembly
I can hear her footsteps tapping as she walks down the corridor
They sound like horses trotting along a road

She looks at me with a mean grin on her face
At that point a ball of red-hot flames burns inside my stomach
This makes me gulp

She drones on and on about discipline and detentions
I start to drift off to sleep
Like a tired newborn puppy

Emma! She calls
I open my eyes
She stares at me
Like an animal looking out for its prey

I am terribly embarrassed
I can feel my face turning red
As if I were a beetroot
Sweat starts to form on my forehead

I hold my head down low
Sorry Miss.

Emma Kelly-Hollin (11)
Graveney School

THE STORM

The day was hot and sultry,
The air was close and heavy,
The grass was drooping and turning brown,
The streams were dried to nought but a trickle.
And then the storm struck.
A crack of lightning heralded the sudden change of weather.
Seconds later the rain followed,
Coming down in torrent upon torrent,
Flattening small plants and grass.
Then more lightning, splitting the sky in two,
Accompanied by deafening thunder.
Then came the wind.
It swept across the open ground,
Buffeting young trees and lashing branches against the tree's trunk.
And it got stronger still, wrenching trees from their roots,
Uprooting bushes and flinging them around as if they
were paper models.
The lightning strikes down tall trees not yet dragged from the
ground by the gale.
Streams burst their banks when they can hold no more rain.
But all of a sudden, as unexpectedly as it had started,
The wind and the rain and the thunder and the lightning stopped dead,
With only its trail of destruction to show it had ever taken place.
The storm is over.

Nicholas Barker (11)
Graveney School

COPY CAT

As sick as I am to say it now,
When I was younger I idolised my brother.
Today I'm lucky if a day passes without a row
And us being pulled apart by our mother.

I'd watch as he smothered his hair in gel,
Or kick a football around the park.
Sometimes I would actually forget I was a girl
And let him gel my hair for a laugh.

I seem to remember, when I was three
Jumping on a toy box; just my brother and me.
We jumped and jumped with me following his moves,
Until he leapt off in horror, leaving me confused.
'Get off Danielle, you're gonna fall through!'
'But Steven,' I cried, 'I'm doing it just like you.'

Do I need to say what happened next?
My lip all torn and my face a mess.
From that day on I went my own way
Which is why I think we are so different today.

Danielle Plummer (16)
Graveney School

ALL SEASONS GRANNY

In the spring when I am 72,
I want to be fit and really *cool*,
I'll dive and splash and jump in a pool,
And embarrass people so they feel like a fool.

In the summer when I am 74,
When my boyfriend comes knocking at the door,
We will venture onto the dance floor,
Where we will *boogie* forever more.

In the autumn when I am 76,
I'll play hopscotch and pick up sticks,
Go to bingo and go to play pool,
Look after grandaughter, fetch her from school.

In the winter when I am 78,
I'll go through the garden to get to the gate,
Rush to the park, hope I am not late,
For a piece of my birthday cake.

Holly Wilson (12)
Grey Coat Hospital School

POEM OF OLD AGE

Dear Nan,

When you're old and feeling grey
for some reason you might say:
    Those were the days and
    Those were the times
So just listen to what's on our minds:
    Football,
    Candy,
    Pocket money too.

But Nan, we will always still love U . . .

Tasha Sinclair (12)
Grey Coat Hospital School

WHEN I'M 64

When I'm 64,
I would not like to be treated any different than anyone younger or older,
Don't dress me in silly *pink* dresses down to my ankles,
And put me in an old people's home for the rest of my life where everyone just sits around all day long doing nothing,
Don't just give me just enough money so I can't even buy myself a proper dinner,
You'll properly still be thinking I can't eat as much as I could 34 years ago, well you'll be wrong.

Let me tell you how I would like to be treated,
First of all with respect,
Not wearing silly *pink* dresses,
But with my Reebok trainers and my Nike tracksuit,
And just a little more money so I can have a proper dinner (for once)
I can look after myself you know, I'm not 2 years old (anymore).

I'm now 64 and you're doing all the things I wished you never would do,
Saying things behind the old lady's back,
(Thinking she can't hear)
Dressing me in silly frilly *pink* dresses,
Putting me in an old ladies home,
And just don't give me just enough money so I can't even get some food,
Well, if I had my own way you'll be sorry.

Tamika Roper (12)
Grey Coat Hospital School

WHEN I'M 64!

When I'm 64 I wanna be cool and hip
I want to be on high like a captain of a cruise ship.
I want to get in trouble with the cops and be on Top of the Pops.

I want to wear clothes with polka dots,
I want to be bad and naughty and smash china pots.
I want to take my grandchildren out clubbing every night.
I want to be rude and maybe pick a fight.
Last of all I'd want to have fun and never regret anything I'd done.

Faye Paget (12)
Grey Coat Hospital School

FRIENDS

Friends are there for you
to keep you from feeling blue.
They make you laugh and smile
and you they don't revile.

They give you loyalty and support.
It doesn't matter if they're tall or short,
or if they're fat or thin.
What counts is what's within.

They comfort you when you're down
and when you need cheering up they'll take you into town.
You treat them with respect
and many friends you will collect.

Kathryn Marle (12)
James Allen's Girls' School

SNAILS AND THEIR SHELLS

Snails
Tentatively taste the air
With their little eyes,
Creeping along
In their egg-crisp
Shells.
They hear the warning
Tremulous footsteps of
Size 8 DMs
But they know their awaited
Fate has come.
Next morning we see their
Flattened remains
Like speckled sputum,
Trapped amongst the tarmac.

Jenny Lau (13)
James Allen's Girls' School

TRAPPED

Here I sit, contained within the walls of chaos,
Where silence cuts through with a sharp, jagged edge,
Where time is unleashed and speeds wildly through
The endless stream of consciousness and rests along the ledge.

While an off-beat pulse is throbbing in my mind,
I search for the door that's just out of my grasp.
As I grope in the dark I can see there is no escape
From the grating hand in which I am clasped.

Trapped.

Sanchia Purkayastha (14)
James Allen's Girls' School

YOU ARE MY LIFE

Standing,
As tall as a mountain.
When angry you are death,
When happy light.
You are plain,
But with your eyes of glass
And lips of blood, you are life.
Casting a motionless shadow over my heart.

Thinking,
Ordinary yet wonderful thoughts,
Of mountain streams,
Bubbling.
The shadow of a tall tree,
Waving.
Plain simple things,
They are you,
You are my life.
You are the light at the end of my tunnel.
As sharp as broken glass,
You cut me,
You break me,
I am gone.

Samantha German (13)
James Allen's Girls' School

SNOBS!

I, have a 60ft yacht,
But it is rather cramped.
Oh I can imagine darling,
My 90ft yacht isn't exactly spacious,
But my Olympic size swimming pool, well.
I'm sure it's lovely, I went for a smaller one,
So I could fit in a jacuzzi,
Which is fabulous sweetie.
Yes, well my Mercedes S needs to be upgraded,
You must know it, the one with,
Automatic windows, air conditioning, radio, CD-player.
Yes I vaguely recall something of that kind,
Oh you've reminded me to phone my chauffeur,
He's supposed to pick me up from the theatre.
Oh really, what are you seeing?
Les Miserables, with my old friend Sir Elton John.
Oh really?
Anyway, I must dash, my private jet's waiting.
Oh that's quite alright, I'm off to see Richard,
He wants me to buy Virgin.

Natasha Nixon (13)
James Allen's Girls' School

CRYSTAL BUTTERFLY

Sitting on my dressing table,
Wings resting,
Eyes desolate and black
Tiny antennae wavering in the wind.

A spectrum of colours reflect on the cloth,
Reds, oranges, yellows, purple,
Bounce off ornaments,
A glint of the sun captured.

Natasha Vowles (12)
James Allen's Girls' School

VOICES IN MY HEAD

I try to block them out.
They speak.
Pushing me.

Never silence,
Always chaos.

It's no use.
I never reply.
It's like a cycle.

Never silence,
Always chaos.

They always return.
They speak again.
I just can't cope.

Never silence,
Always chaos.

Nina McDermott (15)
James Allen's Girls' School

CLOUD

A silver swan drifting,
Gazes down on us.
Guard for the sun,
Gold plated shield.
Formless yet defined
Melt in the mouth candy,
Picked straight from the sky.
Some made like volcanoes.
Big, bellowing, bags of feathers.
Others, made when the witches spring clean,
And sweep the sky.
Unique, and like a snowflake,
Whipped cream spread across the sky.
Perfect in every way
Lonesome wanderers walking the universe,
Searching for a place to settle.

Leili Farzaneh (11)
James Allen's Girls' School

ANIMALS AND HUMANS

The baboon runs onto the pitch,
Kicking the coconut ball.
He calls for his friends.
Orang-utans, monkeys and apes.
Suddenly the cheering of the stadium stops.
Here come the humans,
Shearer, Campbell and Owen.
They are kicking a leather ball.
That was once the baboon's dear friend.

Divya Pande (13)
James Allen's Girls' School

UNTITLED

Wake up at dawn and ask me
Why, with the world stretching out beneath us
All we're sure of is each other.
Struggling
To stay still.

Look at me once more but don't
Smile - if I intrigue you
You know what I'm here for.
Tell me
Don't hold back.

Close your eyes and see
We've come this far
Without letting go.

Sophie Gilbert (15)
James Allen's Girls' School

AUTUMN

Her soft touch,
Turns the luscious green leaves,
Crisp and golden,
Then with one gentle blow,
From her tender brown lips,
They slowly, gracefully fall to the ground,
They turn the floor, once soft and green,
Into a rustling carpet,
Of burning reds and vibrant yellows,
She is the crunch and crackle of autumn.

Victoria Trevelyan (12)
James Allen's Girls' School

STARS

I look outside my window.
I treat my eyes to
    diamonds glittering, shining,
Saying,
'Look here! I'm brighter!'
And yet, far away,
A voice says,
'These stars are suns,
Somewhere out there.'
I think how this light,
Took millions, trillions of years,
To reach our thick, black, velvet sky.
I can see a twinkle here,
    a twinkle there.
I can see a bar, the Ursa Major,
    Cancer and Pegasus.
And then slowly, the stars are
    evaporated from the sky.

Paola Rodriguez (12)
James Allen's Girls' School

TSARIST'S TRIUMPH

The people he met there were touched.
Difficult and mysterious,
Sharp and original,
They echoed with strictness and discipline,
But he softened it with mementoes.
The guttering candles inherited a fine worldly wonder.
He snorted with laughter at the vanished world.

Charlie Parker (12)
James Allen's Girls' School

Football

Football brings me joy.
When I walk onto the field.
It sends a shiver down my spine.
I hear the crowd screaming my name.
The big match is about to start.
One final word with the coach and *Go! Go! Go!*
The whistle has been blown.
The match has started.
I have been passed the ball.
I have a shot at goal.
I've scored!
Two minutes into the game and I scored.
All the other team are climbing on top of me.
The crowd is roaring with happiness.

The score is 1-0 to my team.
There is only one minute left of the game.
I am passed the ball again, I have a shot at goal again.
I've scored again!
Just as the final whistle was blown the ball hit the back of the goal.
My team had won!
2-0 both goals scored by me.
As I shot my second goal.
I felt a shudder of happiness come down my spine
Oh what happiness football brings me!

Stephanie Bartscht (11)
James Allen's Girls' School

NO MORE?

They told me:
It halted, everything.
Movement was still,
Noise was quiet -
She was no more.
I was no more?
Life was no more?
Dead ending?

They told me; again.
Nothing, no more.

Nothing but me;
And her?
But she's no more,
So . . . am I?
Yes,
They say 'Yes.'

Eyes reach out;
Distraction.
The carpet's fraying;
Her cardigan's fraying -
No more.

The carpet is blue?
Or green?
Her eyes are blue?
Or green?
She says green;
They say 'No more.'
I say 'No more?' Then grey.

There are crumbs;
She hates crumbs.
She makes biscuits,
No more biscuits.
Biscuits make crumbs,
No more crumbs.

She will be happy.

No more 'Be'.
They say 'Was'
I say 'Was?'
I say 'Why?'

She frayed;
The biscuits were eaten,
Now she is a crumb.

Natalie Barry (13)
James Allen's Girls' School

MY SPECIAL TREAT

C hocolate is the best of food,
H ot or cold, it changes my mood,
O h how I love to eat
C adbury's and Nestlé as a treat
O range, plain, dark or white. It's just too
L ovely, delicious, so miraculously
    scrumptious it's
A dream
T he taste is the best bit,
E ndlessly eating it.

Sarah Godden (11)
James Allen's Girls' School

On Saturday Morning

On Saturday morning I washed my face,
Wondering how had been my days.

Hear some noise from the kitchen,
Knowing Mother is playing with the dishes.

Quickly dress and run downstairs,
Hoping my breakfast is delicious there.

This time the breakfast is letting me down,
Because the boring style is just around.

Ate my meal and watched the telly,
Why does the nonsence program wait for me?

All my luck ends today,
Will I be able to spend my day?

Dorothy Joe (13)
James Allen Girls' School

I Can't Live Anymore

I had to end my life
I couldn't stay any longer
I knew it was finally time to go
I heard the devil's taunting laughter
Tears ran down my face
Stinging my eyes like acid
My soul broke free
My body was left motionless and yet peaceful
All I had left were my faded memories
My life seemed so pointless
I took a final glimpse at my destiny . . .

Elizabeth Cook (11)
James Allen's Girls' School

MYSELF

My body is crying.
I can hear it.
I'm stirring, struggling, stretching

myself too far.
Recline, rest -

No.
I have not finished
I can still hear it,
I'm sorry.
I can hear the aches and the painful
cry of my body.

Just one more line,

Too much
Can't finish

sleep. But I am awake.

Karen Amoa (14)
James Allen's Girls' School

DEFLATED FOREVER

I feel like a beachball,
Normally cheerful and bright.
But I have a hole,
So, however hard you try I'll never be cheerful
And bright again,
Just useless and deflated.

Catriona Lucas (14)
James Allen's Girls' School

The Universe

It is dark and unknown
Forever timeless
Expanding but shrinking
The space is enveloping.
Stars roar and burn
Giving off heat and light,
While planets hover endlessly and pointlessly
Like dust on a black velvet cloth.
Galaxies shimmer in swirls of light and colour.
Surrounding them is melancholy emptiness
Breathing its long, sighing breath.
It is cold and immortal like a god.
It is eternal.

Sheila Jen (11)
James Allen's Girls' School

Secret

Wrapped in your own emotions you suffer in silence,
Bottling your desire to tell.
You're disorientated and confused,
But you won't try to find out more,
For curiosity killed the cat.
We've been friends too long for you to betray me,
And I know you,
You'll take it to the grave,
To save your own back.

Bridget Whelan (13)
James Allen's Girls' School

OLD

The old woman is like an old machine:
Creaking and stiff with age.
Rusty; like an old bicycle,
The cogs and wheels
That once whirred
And spun eagerly, energetically,
Go slower,
As if bored of working.
Stopping and starting
Irregularly.
Never knowing
If the next stop
Will be the last.
Slower:
Painfully slow.
Trying to make one last feeble   pointless   effort.

Claudia Kemp (15)
James Allen's Girls' School

LIFE

As I sit in this cinema, that we call life,
I watch the moving picture - time.
I reminisce about scenes that should change.
But nothing can seem to be arranged.
Never sure which ticket that you will receive
A bank note, cheque, maybe in debt.
If there was anything to be required,
It would be to know that there is a lot
                to be desired.

Chenat Madziwa (12)
James Allen's Girls' School

UNTITLED

The city's dead at night
It's just me left in the darkness
I stand there in the middle of the garden
Looking at the moon
No one's there to speak to me
And no birds to cheer me up with their songs

And then I suddenly notice,
The horizon is getting lighter
The sun is coming up
The birds waking up
The people starting to go to work
The children shouting, laughing,
But then I notice it's dark again.

Inessa Samokhvalova Goodman (12)
James Allen's Girls' School

ON THE WILD SIDE

The sun shines in at the window bright,
Flooding the room in yellow light.
An old Persian Blue dozes on a bed,
Laying on his paws, his small silky head.
Living a life of nervous lux'ry,
The world outside he cannot see.

A ginger alley cat stands on a shattered wall,
King of all he sees.
All his life he's stood tall,
Living in perfect ease.

Stephanie Williams (11)
James Allen's Girls' School

WHAT'S THAT SHINING?

Silver shadows in the depth of darkness,
Watching her every move,
Catching a glimpse of her eye,
Or the twitching, twitching, twitching.

Softly, she tenderly tiptoes towards her goal,
There it is, big and bright,
But, what is that shining?
What is that glistening, glistening, glistening?

She creeps up,
Right up close,
And watches in the moonlight,
She is staring, staring, staring, staring.

She goes for the snatch,
... *snap!*
The trap has got her,
She is gone, gone, gone.

Amelia Scott (12)
James Allen's Girls' School

UNTITLED

They fly at night when no one's around,
By trees, in forests they hang upside down,
They use their radar since they can't hear a sound.
Not red nor green but either black or brown.

These fly at midday, when it's hot and dry,
On flowers or plants they can be found.
But if you try catching them, they'll just fly by,
Multicoloured but still no distinctive sound.

Sheena Patel (12)
James Allen's Girls' School

ICARUS

The blue wonder stretches before us.
The father's word and then a rush
Of sudden air as we launch.
The blue wonder is coming closer,
But as my wings begin to beat
It slows down and stops.
Now it is going away,
I can look down on it
And feel the power of flying.
The glorious power
Of flying with the birds,
Looking down on the world
And seeing the yellow
Twinkling against the blue.
Even Helios himself seems so close
I could fly up and talk to him
And drive in his magnificent chariot.
Enough power to feel as a god.
Someone below me calls my name
But I cannot respond.
I must reach Helios,
I must, I must.
I have!
A face looks at me
With anger and pity mixed.
Now I have stopped.
It is forbidden.
I fall,
I fall towards Poseidon,
The blue wonder ever closer
And I forget.

Leonie Stone (14)
James Allen's Girls' School

DEATH

An innocent walk in the woods,
Only the distant hooting of an owl breaks the golden silence,
The trees stand as still as a lion watching its prey,
Watching it as though it has no chance of survival -
Suddenly a premonition occurs.

A sharp pain right through me,
The blade glistens like the reflection of the moon in a river,
Hearing footsteps hurrying through the rustling leaves,
I know my life is at an end.

I fall to the ground,
Blood trickling from my heart,
My eyes slowly flicker until they shut -
Shut firmly like a prison door, never to open again.

Purni Patel (14)
James Allen's Girls' School

MY ETERNAL FRIEND

A perfect being
Ebony complexion
Dressed in classic black
Of her disposition I have no clue
So graceful
So quiet
So loyal
Although absent still present
A chameleon changing with mood
Sometimes grey, maybe black, purple or blue.

Aletia Aston (15)
James Allen's Girls' School

SECRETS

Behind a door, all nooks and crannies,
Lives a box, dark brown with dust on the top.
It holds my memories of childhood,
These secrets nobody knows.

The secrets of joy and sadness,
Locked away with a golden key,
The key which nobody has.
Lost.

These secrets I once hid in my mind,
I was a child when I held these secrets,
And now I dream of opening the chest,
The chest of secrets.

Alice Mackay (12)
James Allen's Girls' School

DREAMING

I'm here again,
The place of my rest,
The colours all bright,
No problems lie beneath my skin,
The soundless laughing of people
Playing, being happy, feeling free
My eyes reluctantly open,
I awaken from my dreams,
I breathe once more.
The heavy dark breath of
Loneliness and isolation,
Until my sleep once again
Sets my mind free.

Jasmine Patel (15)
James Allen's Girls' School

MURDERESS

A distant shout echoes in the dark,
Sending cold ripples of fear through her.
Her hesitant footsteps frightened to mark,
The cold hard ground before her.

Darkness lingering around every turn,
Unable to escape the shadows cast.
Although alone, she feels the cold eyes burn
Through her, her steps become fast.

But whose eyes could be staring?
She was certain she was alone.
Did they want the secret she was bearing,
To unravel the lies that were unknown?

She rushed through the graveyard,
Her movement lost in stress,
She cried, her whipped soul strained hard,
She left, a cold murderess.

Maria-Louisa Norris (14)
James Allen's Girls' School

CHOCOLATE

Children love it,
Hot or cold.
Orange tang,
Caramel taste,
Oh, can't wait!
Lick your lips in a mouth-watering sensation.
At last I get to eat it!
Taste that chocolate,
Ever wanting more.

Tanya Lake (11)
James Allen's Girls' School

BAZAAR

The smell of burning incense snakes through the air
Coursing like blood through the veins of the night
Like a pulse rate the bongo drums steadily beat
Interrupted by chatter or stamping of feet.
And clay masks in hideous grimaces stare
Like callous black eyes in silent despair
And the jostling people who're dressed in their best
Are laughing, or angry, or crazy from drink.
Smells of Malibu, Coke and cigarette smoke
Are fighting like germs with the crisp air of night.
Silver jewellery hangs from the stalls like salt tears
And it glints in the light of the burnt-orange stars.
Webs of tradesmen with skin coloured chocolate brown
Sing a bargaining song with their punters or friends
And their smocks, which are dyed in the hues of the sun
Billow gently, caught out by the breezes of night.

Above this lively body a canopy lies
Of thick plush black velvet bestudded with jewels
And I walk through the worn cobbled streets with my friend
Holding onto her soft silky hazelnut arm
And we look at the stalls, and we drink cans of Coke
And we're cells in the body that's wrapped in night's cloak.

Olivia Stredder (14)
James Allen's Girls' School

SISTER, YOUNGER SISTERS

Younger sisters, they're a pain.
Whenever you go somewhere
They're regularly late,
And even when they are ready,
They always forget something!
Her appearance is appalling!
Hair's a mess, shoes undone,
Always clashing never matching.
When friends come over she never ceases at being silly
And when they aren't there, she's just downright annoying.
She's constantly hyper
(I think she keeps a stash of sugar in her room.)
And always pushes my button on just the right spot.
But even though through all her faults
(and many more)
I love her and she's *my* sister.

Julia Nawrocki (12)
James Allen's Girls' School

AWAITING DINNER

The smells entice the palate
And taunt the senses.
The wonder and anticipation
Of what lies bubbling behind that door,
The odour seeping out like thin tendrils of fog,
And then the door is opened
And the excitement ends.

Sarah Castor-Perry (12)
James Allen's Girls' School

Torosay, Isle Of Mull, August 1998

The vast mansion
Rooms restored.
Dating back,
To the Victorians.

The giant beds,
High ceilings
Beautiful carvings,
A wide patio.

The well-tended garden,
Neat rows of flowers.
Perfectly trimmed bushes,
A tumbling fountain.

Arches of roses
Leading back and back.
Through every colour,
To an ivy-covered fence.

Behind it is wilderness,
Neglected for years.
Home to the scavengers,
Overtaken by weeds.

Left, as its own master,
Disturbed by no human,
Invisible to the world,
Hidden from visitors.

Not a part of the elaborate corridors,
The perfect rows of flowers,
So unchanged since the period.
The only real Victorian.

Jessica-Ann Jenner (12)
James Allen's Girls' School

SILENCE

A ladybird walking slowly across a leaf,
An artist at work on a masterpiece painting,
An owl swooping to the ground to catch its prey,
And a star shooting through the night sky.

The slow development of an unborn child,
The darkness of night closing in on the world,
The brain working to find the answer,
And the earth slowly spinning around the sun.

Deaf people communicating with their hands,
Tree roots pushing their way through soil,
Smoke curling out from a chimney pot,
And eyes focusing on the pages of a book.

All these things happen,
But they all happen in silence.

Chloe Hayward (12)
James Allen's Girls' School

UNTITLED

A whistle goes,
The end is near.
A bird flies overhead.
The shadow casts some doubt
About the world below
An endless day.
An hour gone.

Polly Davidson (15)
James Allen's Girls' School

POEM

For English tonight I have a poem,
I thought of Keats - but didn't know 'im,
So I will have to be the poet,
Although you'll never truly know it.
It's hard for words to be expressed,
It really makes me quite depressed,
To write that kind of po-et-ry
It creates a big difficulty.
What kind of poem should I write?
I'm never going to get it right.
Thank God for that I'm nearly through,
My hand is sore it's going blue,
This little poem has no meaning,
If I don't stop now, I'll end up . . . *screaming!*

Josephine Pell (14)
James Allen's Girls' School

WORKING MOTHER

Wreckless abandonment, selfish desire;
Play with the matches get burnt by the fire.
Unstable, unsturdy, on a pedestal stood;
A hand to the stars reaching higher and higher.

Habit clad oyster, in gushing stream;
Clutching and snatching at jewels unseen.
Pearls of pure gold, fragile yet bold,
Pupils glazed over with green.

Your eyes, a soft breeze on the looks of stern stone;
You are my own, from my rib, from my bone.
I know that the apron won't ever fit snug,
Yet, my love, you are never alone.

Efua Mercer (15)
James Allen's Girls' School

GOSSIP

'Who?'
'What?'
'Where?'
'When?'
'Really!'
'Never!'
'How could they?'
'Oh terrible!'
All these words and a lot, lot more,
Can be heard from behind the parlour room door.
The mistress is baffled
The master's aghast,
And the butler knows more,
But will not tell all,
Of what is being said about last week's ball.
The cook is mixing a gossip concoction
A mixture of truth and lies.
The maids add snippets and morsels aplenty,
About who just might be the baker's new bride.
The gossip is caught like a mouse by a hawk,
When the kitchen staff listen to idle men's talk.
So there's one thing I'm sure one should always ignore,
And that's what is said behind the parlour room door.

Laura Whitehead (14)
James Allen's Girls' School

CREATION

Sun rising over the horizon.
Waves forming from crimson tides,
Crashing unstoppingly against cliff sides.
The harmonious music of wind blowing.

Morning rises, sleep comes no more.
The bathroom, your favourite room to explore.
Days pass by without a sound,
The flowing of the Red Sea carelessly forgotten.

Bright stars explore the darkened night;
Icing specks on a double chocolate cake.
Taste heightened by urging impulses.
The new form ascends.

The rolling hills burdened with fluid.
Pastures green and sky a blue.
Tree branches grow bigger, the trunk bares no support;
Aches and pains soothed by . . .

. . . *Thud!* - The sound of thunder in a storm.
Reckless assumption, think twice.
Underestimated movement
A scared little girl; her first storm.

Draped curtains across the sceen play.
Dignity must be upheld throughout;
Image is nothing, pride is everything
Created from passion, the fruit grows.

The darkened night holds the house of horrors.
A sharp ray of light,
The dark double chocolate cake;
How to resist? Temptation is high.

Why restrain yourself, you deserve it.
Months of two in one coming to an end,
Time for seperation is near.
Trees gone and rolling hills now mounds.

Waterfalls crash to an open grave.
The fruit of passion has bloomed into a flower.
I can se it ahead, teardrops fall,
Creator of life has succeeded.

Temitope Popoola (15)
James Allen's Girls' School

CLIFF JUMP

I stand on the edge.
My legs are like rubber
That I struggle to control.
I tilt dangerously forwards,
Dizzy with excitement.
The clear, turquoise water
Sparkles beneath me,
Calm and still.
Without knowing how,
I jump.
My mind is blank
Then the reality dawns on me -
I am falling, falling.
It is all over in a flash.
I hit the blueness.
A tingling sensation
Floods my body
As I plunge
Into the depth of the ocean.

Elizabeth Lim (14)
James Allen's Girls' School

The Ghost

As I laid my head to sleep,
A cold breeze filled the room.
I rose and looked around,
And there, in the corner,
Sat a faint figure of a girl.
Her clothes were white,
And her face pale and withered.
Her long, brown whispy hair,
Blew across her face.
Her eyes, filled with fear,
Pleaded for help.
As I moved closer, to comfort her,
She faded away.
All that remained was the dark corner
                which was there before.
Who was she?
Why had she come to me?
How can I help her?
Help her leave this world.

Rosie Simmons (15)
James Allen's Girls' School

Sick/Sad/Pathetic

Hello disease, yes it's me again.
You knew that I'd come back to you
Although you knew not when.
Happiness has perished, burnt by your cold flame.
I could not cope with difficult hope;
I missed your easy pain.

Your harsh love is my comfort,
The only thing I know.
Your slow abuse is my excuse,
My lover and my foe.
I let myself be taken,
Like someone lost at sea
At the beckon of the ocean
To its cold, dark peace.

Hannah Battershell (14)
James Allen's Girls' School

WHAT DO YOU WANT?

What do you want?
I don't want to see you,
Go away, now, and leave me alone.

Don't even touch me, get out of here,
I can't bear to watch you,
Why have you come?

I don't want to talk, don't even try to,
You know I can't stand you,
Get out, or I'll scream.

OK, it's your last chance, get out of my sight,
Don't even try to explain
Shut the door when you leave.

The room is empty,
It's late at night.
It's cold and I'm frightened,
Please come back.

Sasha Milavic Davies (14)
James Allen's Girls' School

MEMORIES

As I walked through the night,
I thought I'd never see the light.
From the time I saw you die,
For you I would always cry.

But now I know,
Someone can change my life.
When you reached for that knife,
I could never turn my head when
I saw the blood on your bed.

The memories come back,
But the happiness I lack
I will still remember you,
No matter what, Adieu!

Marina Harnik (12)
James Allen's Girls' School

JAGS

First year means long skirts, obedience and more
Second year means bickering and friends galore
Third year means cockiness and loud at all times
Fourth year means displeasure at the third year's crimes
Fifth year means worry, you're big girls now
Lower sixth means homework and social life
                              To balance it - how?
Upper sixth means A levels and exiting the school
On to University to learn more rules.

Georgina Warren (15)
James Allen's Girls' School

A Cage

A cage holds me powerless,
I cannot think,
My heart pours out emotions,
Which I cannot feel.

Seeing my friends hurt,
Trying to reach out but not touching,
Seeing everyone frightened, ill and hungry,
I am stuck inside a cage not being able to help.

I beat against the thick iron bars,
The bars that hold me in this prison,
I try to feel what other people are feeling,
I try to find my own feelings but they are lost somewhere
In my heart.

I sit in my cage,
And slowly a tear trickles down my face.

Caitlin Albery Beavan (12)
James Allen's Girls' School

Broken Collarbone

Trapped in my sling
Like a tiger in its cage,
Looking outwards.

To the casual world before me
I am a stranger,
Feeling despair.

I am free yet imprisoned
And I'll never forget this.
I am waiting.

Christine Szekely (15)
James Allen's Girls' School

GUILT

She's in the wrong and everyone knows
She's feeling bad, and it certainly shows
She tries to hide
From the unrest inside

She's feeling proud
Yet she is allowed
To free her mind of pain,
She'll never do it again . . .

The world is against her
Constantly condemning her
For that one stupid deed
Will her anguish ever be freed?

To turn back the clock would be all too good
To think about the past leaves her misunderstood
How on earth could she be so naïve?
Why not pack her bags, and simply leave?

No one forgives her, or forgets that lie
No one wants to hear her stupid alibi
Why did she do it? What should she do?
Why, it's quite simply up to you!

Rosalind Tew (15)
James Allen's Girls' School

UNIDENTIFIED SHINING OBJECTS

Glowing like a newborn star,
  Dark and darker up above,
Crescent shaped, indescribable,
  Like a night light in the sky.

Even more bright lights beyond,
  Smaller than the newborn star,
Hundreds, thousands, seem uncontrolled,
  Paint sprinkled on black paper.

Sandra Djokic (12)
James Allen's Girls' School

RUSH HOUR IN DULWICH

Mothers with children in giant spacewagons,
Battle with others to drive their darlings to school,
Even though they live next to the places,
It's a power drive and they have to rule!

The worst mums are those who insist,
On dropping their babes in the middle of the road,
Stopping traffic to give them a kiss,
While other drivers' tempers erode!

Coaches full and buses too,
Grinding to a halt,
Watching that lot driving through,
Is enough to start a revolt!

Angry businessmen heading for the city
Glare at the Dulwich mums,
They do not think to pity,
The weary children being put through the humdrum!

And then we see sensibly walking by,
Amidst the noise and grime,
Those who choose to use their feet,
And therefore save much time!

Katie Prescott (15)
James Allen's Girls' School

UNITED IN DEATH

In a country of perpetual ice and wind,
He was born.
To a doting mother and father,
Who believed and hoped he would be great.

He now wears khaki.

In a country which frost had never touched,
A boy was born.
His parents loving and adoring him,
They wanted to give him the best future they could.

He now salutes a general.

They both saluted a senior officer,
Were both waved and cheered off,
With handkerchiefs and tears in the same way,
Even though they called each other enemy.

They both fired at each other
Snipers, bullets, shells,
They both went over the top and met,
Face to face, rifle to rifle.

They are now both united in death.

Amna Ahmad (13)
James Allen's Girls' School

A FRIEND

A friend is there for you when you need them,
To share secrets and to have fun with.
When you are in doubt you go to them and you
Sort it through,
They're always there to help you.

When you're sad they cheer you up,
When someone teases you they stick up for you,
You do things together,
And you need to be nice to them too.

Eliza Ward (11)
James Allen's Girls' School

TO MY BABY SISTER

In a baby castle,
just beyond my eye,
my baby plays with angel toys
that money cannot buy.
Who am I to wish her back
into this world of strife?
No, play on, my baby
you have eternal life.

At night when all is silent,
and sleep forsakes my eyes,
I'll hear her tiny footsteps
come running to my side.
Her little hand caresses me
so tenderly and sweet,
I'll breathe a prayer and
close my eyes,
and embrace her in my sleep.

Now I have a treasure
I rate above all other,
I have known one glory -
as now I have another.

Sahra Janmohamed (15)
James Allen's Girls' School

Paradise

The sun shone down quite wondrously,
With colourful beams aglow,
And all was silent yet filled with peace
And reverence was all on show.

The air was filled with ecstasy,
Beauty was all around,
Peace and wonder anointed my heart;
I was quite spellbound.

Paradise is not known now,
The air is caressed in hate.
Terror and grudges are known too well;
Pain and death are about.

But let us be thankful that we are alive
And rejoice in our being here today.
Let us face the facts - life is good,
In every single way.

Life was glorious in the days of that paradise,
With the shimmering wonder of living.
A warm glow lay in every heart,
Fondling each moment of truth.

The feeling in that paradise was amazing,
But let us begin anew.
'Animal rights' and 'Save the world!'
There is much work for us to do!

Jessie Smart (11)
James Allen's Girls' School

THE JOURNEY

Flashing blue lights,
Grey tarmac far ahead
Sixty, seventy, no eighty
The spinning dial read.

Lights nearby,
There is comfort here,
But the darkness engulfs me
And then comes fear.

Crash of steel
Screaming in sight,
Twisted bodies,
Blood glimmering in light.

No, red car, blue car
Street lights
Green fields
This is real, this is right.

Like the sky
On a starry night
Out of the darkness in front of me
Comes shimmering light.

My fears are gone,
The darkness fades
There is no crash
My journey is made.

Laura McCahery (14)
James Allen's Girls' School

PRE-MID LIFE CRISIS

I'm twenty-eight and a failure
And no more paths to take,
My career's down the toilet
I've no more hearts to break.

It's stupid I let that bloke go
When he could have been 'the one',
I guess I as too hung up on the fact
That I'd only just dumped his son.

I'm over bars and pubs now
They're just no longer my scene,
The atmosphere seems wrong somehow
Unless you're seventeen.

My sister's happily married
Her life's all figured out
I'm doing something wrong somehow
Of that I'm in no doubt.

Maybe I will die lonely
A spinster past her prime,
All alone in a cold bedsit
P'raps life's just a waste of time.

Rebecca Clarke (15)
James Allen's Girls' School

HOLD ON TO FRIENDSHIP

Why does she desert me,
And pretend to not know?
I feel a weep inside of me,
But do not want to show.

I wish she would hold out her hand,
And make me feel at ease.
For friendship is a glowing delight,
That she should catch and seize.

Zoë Abrahams (13)
James Allen's Girls' School

DREAMING

The dream has come again.
Every night it hits me,
like a dagger piercing any hope of peace.

I dread silence now.
Before it was a place of beauty;
a place so golden that only
I could feel the pure ecstasy of it.

Now it fills me with dread,
dread of the inevitable.
The dread of my dream.

I fear darkness, the feeling of calm
one feels before they slip into a slumber.

For now I know that only when I'm still,
only then it can reach me,
swallow me up and take me away,
away to the land of destruction.
Destruction of hope and truth.

Last night the dream came again.

Florence McHugh (14)
James Allen's Girls' School

OLD LADIES

What are old ladies,
Older versions of us.
Some are extravagant,
Some just make a fuss.

Some are worriers,
Money, health, anything at all.
Some are unusual
And just like having a ball.

Their wrinkled faces,
From stress and ageing.
Their pace is unhurried,
As if time is slowing.

And old ladies seem to be in
A world that's stopped moving,
Around thirty odd years ago.
But the world is not revolving
Around them but beside them
              behind them
                  in front of them.

Kate Rodney (13)
James Allen's Girls' School

YOUNG AND OLD

When I was young,
Life was good and so much fun.
But when I grew,
No one knew,
How much stress they put me through.

Gemma Ford (16)
James Allen's Girls' School

DHARMA

I opened the door,
And in it ran,
A flash of lightning,
All black and tan.

How did it get here?
Where's it from?
Far away?
I could be wrong.

It stole my heart,
I was filled with joy,
I wanted to keep it,
But it's not a toy.

The policeman melted,
When he caught a glance,
It had done no wrong,
But found us by chance.

We walked home,
Without our boss,
We saw the notice,
About her loss.

It took a phone call,
To bring her home,
And grateful owners,
Make offers of loan.

A new friend, Dharma,
To walk in the park,
The Border Collie,
Who stole my heart.

Megan Fisher (14)
James Allen's Girls' School

The Accident

Running, slipping, falling,
Hand held out,
Glass shattered,
Pain floods through my hand,
Deep red blood runs down my wrist,
Blood, panic,
Nervous laughter.
Friends calling,
Taking me away from the bloody scene,
Sink filling with diluted blood,
Bandage wrapped around,
I'm laughing,
It's over,
And I am safe.

Ellie Davies (14)
James Allen's Girls' School

At The Playground

Round and round goes the roundabout
Up and down the swing,
The children, they just run around,
They care not for a thing.

Their mothers they just sit there,
Gossiping like old maids,
Only stopping to glance about,
And see their children stray.

When it's time to leave,
The children, how they cry,
It makes you laugh to see,
How they wave goodbye.

Round and round goes the roundabout,
Up and down the swing,
The children, they just run around,
They care not for a thing.

Jackie Steward (16)
James Allen's Girls' School

A CHILD'S NIGHT

The big bright stars in the sky,
All the young children in bed they lie,
Tucked up with their blankets and small teddy bears,
On their own or sometimes in pairs.
If they're in pairs you might hear small whispers,
They might be brothers, friends or even sisters.
Some sleep with a light on which is ever so bright,
Some sleep with it off, nothing in sight.
They may sleep curled up with an innocent face,
Or spread out or sleeping in an unusual place.
Some may creep downstairs to get a drink
And make a huge noise in the sink.
Some might have a terrifying nightmare,
Which might give them a tremendous scare.
They might go to their parents' room and say,
'Mummy can I sleep in your bed today?'

Nicola Garland (12)
James Allen's Girls' School

OCTAVIA

Her deep, melancholy eyes merge into a grubby face,
Young with bulbous cheeks of adolescence,
But aged by her lifetime of menial tasks,
Dark matted hair falls around her
Like a dirty waterfall streaming with blood.

As she moves, her attire follows her,
A mauve skirt - hitched up at the waist
But still trailing behind the short,
Stocky figure of this young gypsy girl.

Disappearing into the caravan, she emerges
Clutching a slice of ripe watermelon,
Glistening in the last beams of the evening sun
Which fades into a mellow smear of twilight.

She relishes the succulent melon as she sits
Pensive, with an expression of satisfaction,
Juice sliding down her sculpted face,
Brown arms, to her large, tattered shirt.

Cross-legged on the uncut grass, a shawl
Draped round her weary shoulders as the breeze
Sweeps in, a mellifluous tune flows from her fingers,
as she strums on a resounding mandolin.
Rocking in her lap, a lullaby which sends
Her golden puppy into a heavy slumber.

Octavia is her name.

Lucy Anne Hutchinson (14)
James Allen's Girls' School

REALMS OF INSANITY

In Loch Ness they have Nessy,
The Loch Ness monster queen.
In the Alps there is a yeti,
Who's hardly ever seen.

In Hong Kong there's a dragon,
With green and silver toes.
Mister Lear had a dong,
With a brightly glowing nose.

In reality these beings
Are really not that weird.
They're just misunderstood,
And nothing to be feared.

Old Nessy's just a creature,
From the dawn of man.
The land life didn't suit her,
So to the loch she swam.

The yeti's not a yeti,
He's a climber from Madrid.
His family gave him hassle,
So in the Alps he hid.

About the dragon and the dong,
You really must be told.
The dragon's just a gecko,
And the dong's just got a cold.

Now I've told you the bare facts,
You can take them all and file 'em.
But the drugs are wearing off,
So it's back to the asylum.

Abigail Zeitlin (15)
James Allen's Girls' School

A Long Night

I've been told to write a poem
It doesn't have to rhyme
It can be about anything I want
I'm wandering humorous or sublime.

I'm usually not good with poems
Never know what to write
I sit for ages, tapping my fingers
Knowing it'll be a long night

Then my brain starts to work
Inspiration flows
The page starts to fill with ink
As my proud face glows

The poem at last is finished
After a tedious long night
I let out a sigh of relief
As I slowly turn off the light.

Amy Fitzpatrick (14)
James Allen's Girls' School

Icarus Poem

I looked down, my feet were on the edge,
My father's words were in my head,
Don't fly down near the water,
Nor up near the sun.

The ground was lost below me,
We flew like I'd never seen a bird fly.
Then my eye caught the sun,
I seemed to be drawn in by it.

I looked down, the water was far below me,
My father's words were slipping out of my head,
I had to touch the sun,
I couldn't control myself as I flew up.

I suddenly became weaker as hot raindrops,
Fell from me, my wax was melting,
My wings would not move,
I began to fall, very fast . . .

Megan Warwick (15)
James Allen's Girls' School

NEW FRIENDS

It was quiet and serene
Joan came up
'Want to be friends?'
After that we were like hens
Nothing could separate us

Strutting around the playground
Heads held high
We were known as the animal enthusiasts
Always happy with each other's company

Until Isabelle the vixen came . . .

But then there is the girl with urban curls
I think her name is Suzie Earls.

Celeste Tobias-Freitag (11)
James Allen's Girls' School

MARKING EXAMS

The teacher with a pile of papers
Is sitting at her desk.
Writing things like 'very good' or
'I know you tried your best.'
Then suddenly she makes a face
And covers the page in pen,
I know it's mine she's marking
Loads of mishaps to amend.
At all the subjects, every one
I know how bad I am.
Even if I study hard
For all of the exams.
I'm just the kind of person
With no memory at all.
And just like every summer
I've gone and blown them all.

Polly Southern (13)
James Allen's Girls' School

FRIENDS

You know me,
Everything about me.
My secrets, fears, hopes and dreams,
Best friends since we were small.
Inseparable, together always,
Through tough times and sad times,
Happy times and funny times,
Always there for me,
When I needed you.

Helen Wade (12)
James Allen's Girls' School

AUTUMN TO WINTER

The colourful autumn leaves fall to the ground.
The sun shines warmly down not making a sound.
Whilst the squirrels are scuttling around,
                the birds are singing sweetly.
The hedgehogs are getting ready to hibernate,
For the perishing winter's date.

That date has come!
The sun fades,
No more bright rays!
The hedgehogs have hidden,
and the squirrels have away ridden.
The snow like a covering net,
The winter has set!

Natalie Yakimiuk (12)
James Allen's Girls' School

UNTITLED

It was sex, drugs, rock and roll
Now it seems everyone is on the dole
Hippies travelling in the vans
One hand on the horn, the other grasping beer cans
Colours flash, blue, yellow, red, orange, white
Peace man . . . yeah right
What has happened to the good old days?
Now happiness is only where money pays
So now as I slap on my anti-ageing cream
Oh yes, I hear you think how supreme
I think back to the good old days
Where sex, drugs, rock and roll were the ways.

Milly Jarvis (14)
James Allen's Girls' School

HEDGEHOG HOUSE

There is a house in the garden,
But humans don't live there,
It's for some little creatures,
With lots of prickly hair.

This house is made from wood,
They crawl in through the door,
It's quite warm inside,
With comfy leaves on the floor.

They make themselves at home
And share the slugs around,
They're safely hidden there,
Where they can't be found.

But every winter I creep up there,
And look in through the door,
I see a pile of brown conker shells,
Fast asleep on the floor.

Letitia Barry (12)
James Allen's Girls' School

FRIENDS

They're there for you when you're happy,
They're there for you when you're sad.
They share the good times with you,
And help you through the bad.

They listen to all your problems,
They listen to you moan.
They chatter to you all day at school,
Then they talk to you again on the phone.

They argue with you on occasions,
But always come back to make up.
They give you advice in dilemmas,
And help you with work if you're stuck.

Friends are a thing to be treasured,
A good friendship lasts forever.
And when you are old, grey and wrinkly,
You'll still be laughing together.

Rachel Russell (13)
James Allen's Girls' School

THE WILD MUSTANG

Wild mustang scatter across the plain,
The wild horses are here again.
Muscular legs galloping fast,
I wish to have that liberty,
As I watch them racing past.

As they trot over stones,
Their hooves clatter.
They have free wills,
Nothing seems to matter.

Now at last they've stopped to graze,
The leading stallion raises his head and neighs
The rest of the herd start calling out,
They all sense some sort of danger about.
It's the humans coming fast on horseback,
The cowboys kick the horses' sides,
And pull hard at the reins,
Now the wild horses are off again.

Lucy Merrell (11)
James Allen's Girls' School

HIM

The hurting of your sorrow,
The dwelling on the past;
Why did he destroy you?
You thought that it would last.

When troubles were on top of you
He'd always give advice.
But now that it's all over
You feel he stole your life.

The way that he would talk to you
With everlasting words,
You thought you'd be forever
But he shattered your safe world.

He wasn't just your lover
But also your best friend.
You never dreamed that someday
It all would have to end.

When was he coming home that night?
You didn't have a clue,
Until that devastating call
That split your world in two.

They said he never had a chance
When that car went through the light.
He was bringing you some flowers,
To cheer you up that night.

You will never feel his kiss again,
Or his arms to hold you tight.
You can see his face still in your mind.
Why did it have to end that night?

Laura Cooper (12)
James Allen's Girls' School

The Flower

Starting from a tiny seed,
It grows up from the ground,
A little sun, a little rain,
Makes it flourish all year round.

It comes in many colours,
Making the garden bright,
With emerald green, and scarlet red,
Radiant in the deep sunlight.

In the winter, petals fade,
Going yellow, green and brown,
Falling down upon the ground.

Melissa Lawrence (12)
James Allen's Girls' School

The Fire

The fire is lit.
It bursts into a frenzy of blazing excitement and spreads out uncontrollably.
The ferocious flames flicker and break into a furious rage.
Destruction is inevitable.
The flames glow with anger and overpower all.
Everything is a victim.
Nothing survives.
The odour of burning matter is pungent.
There is nothing to be seen,
All is burnt, not a soul remains.
It smokes and smoulders for an age,
Then finally rests leaving a path of annihilation
                                        behind it.

Lily Arnold (13)
James Allen's Girls' School

WHEN WORDS RUN DRY

Once the art of running words
Smoothly, onto the page
Was easy. Now time has passed
And I am gone from that marvellous age.

Long ago, my thoughts were easy
To convey. Now trapped inside
Of me, they are sheltered, protected.
They find it too easy to hide.

And when expressions run as dry
As emotions out of me,
It is futile even to try
To seek inspiration in a tree.

So maybe when I am forced
To surrender my precious art,
I will do so quite sedately
But in doing so break my heart.

Alex Parsons (13)
James Allen's Girls' School

LADIES PAINTING - FRANCE 1860S

The ladies, their hands move quite freely,
The brushes not slowly nor fast.
The ladies, their faces shaded by hats,
Their eyes demurely downcast.

Their dresses of blue, grey or cream,
Swirl round them as they observe and see,
An image by which they feel inspired
A statue, lake or perhaps a tree.

Their paintings, replicas of images,
Frozen moments in time.
Waiters with trays of cut crystal glasses,
Glasses of tonic and lime.

They understand the harmony,
The stillness of the moment,
A tiny world of sheer perfection,
A brief second from heaven sent.

Alex Cairns (13)
James Allen's Girls' School

HATRED

The sweet, strong smell of coffee fills the air,
The scent of freshly baked bread flows through the house,
These pungent smells haunt me every day;
The things I find odious others find marvellous.

I wake up to a bright summer's morning,
Full of ravishing trees and flowers of all colours,
I see these sights every summer;
The things I despise, mesmerise others.

The refreshing taste of mint completes every meal,
Sweet, soothing chocolate melts in my mouth,
I dread these sickly flavours day and night.
The things that make me feel queasy others find yummy.

The harmonious singing of the birds in the morning,
The rustle of leaves on an autumn day,
These sounds and sights are in every season.
People's idea of heaven is my idea of hell.

Keshvi Prajapati (13)
James Allen's Girls' School

THE GRAVEYARD OF CARAVANS

Overlooking the sea
On top of the hill,
Sits the graveyard of caravans
Silent and still.

Once full of life,
Excitement and play,
Now catatonic
Day after day.

A uniform of rust
In orderly lines,
Like mould covered tombs
Decaying with time.

Resurrection impossible,
No one to share,
The death of the caravans.
Does anyone care?

Natasha Almuli (14)
James Allen's Girls' School

THE STORM

The waves are smashing against the beach,
The rain beats the bare rock,
The wind whistles across the ice blue of the water,
And now in the distance lightning strikes,
Then the thunder,
Now silence,
Calm,
The storm is gone.

Alex Mathias (13)
James Allen's Girls' School

ACHIEVEMENT THROUGH DIFFICULTY

Difficulty is a horrible thing,
It carries anger and frustration within,
From things such as playing a game,
Or trying to remember a name!
From trying to master chess,
Or making an accurate guess,
With a whole heap of stress,
And not an ounce of rest,
We may all go ballistic,
But be realistic,
Without this burden,
This great big hurdle,
Where would we be?
Few know the key,
And I think I know,
How to expand and grow,
With difficulty of course,
Like a saddle and a horse,
It goes with aiming,
In that way gaining,
Because in the end,
We won't go around the bend,
Because nothing comes with ease,
If you want to achieve.

Yasmin Hasan (14)
James Allen's Girls' School

EUTHANASIA

Your lurid thoughts are scaring me,
Evasive, skilful, pale.
A whitened lustrous, silent scene,
A purity turned stale.

Evoking darkened, desperate fears,
You slowly choose the scent.
You follow shallow paths of tears,
And wait for my dissent.

Malevolently you live your dreams,
As malice eats you now.
You're dripping with servility,
And sweat falls from your brow.

Don't speak another word to me,
Or try to understand.
I'm out here on my own, I'm free,
Erratic voodoo-land.

In prayers I wish that you could care,
And show you aren't ashamed,
To look at me without despair,
Just gaze, my life is chained.

Your thoughts shall be no longer mine,
You read into my soul.
You want to listen, have no time,
And something takes its toll.

Sarah Enderby (14)
James Allen's Girls' School

THE MEMORY

Hordes of eager tourists scatter the beach,
Tempted by the shining, bright, beaming sun,
By the clear blue sea and the cloudless sky.
She sits among them, small and meaningless,
Gazing at the sparkling sea ahead.
Her eyes do not see, her ears do not hear
The sound of splashing and laughing children.
She remembers, a buried memory.

She rises to her feet, stands tall and proud
But a turmoil of anguish and sorrow
Strives and toils to seize control within her.
Silently she moves through the hushed mourners,
She steps before the simple wooden box.
A grey, darkened sky and dull, lifeless sea,
A biting wind howls unmercifully,
Bringing with it the bitter taste of brine,
And wisps the priest's gowns about his body.
So still she stood, a pillar of stone,
A handful of earth, the moment is gone.
The chill, bleak, waiting hole swallows the box.
She feels a drop of rain upon her face.

The touch of the welcoming sun wakes her,
A teardrop slowly trickles down her face.
She rose and left the beach thronging with life,
Bustling with families on holiday.
She never remembered again.

Clare Cheeseman (14)
James Allen's Girls' School

WHISPER

What is that whisper of hope in your mind,
That is yours and yours alone?
A whisper only dreamers have,
That is kept beneath your bones.

A ray of light, a light of joy
That is concealed from others;
Man, woman, girl and boy,
From all the world's dear brothers.

If my life was to flee away
And drift through the Earth's beams,
I would not care for life that day
For they could never steal my dreams.

Magdalena Powell (14)
James Allen's Girls' School

NEVILLE

There was a hamster called Neville,
He was my favourite hamster
I nicknamed him gangster
For he never put up his paws,
Or gave up his sword,
He was into using guns.
He joined the army to have some fun,
He pumped the iron,
And ground the dirt,
And got a cool green army shirt!

Sophie White (13)
James Allen's Girls' School

THE BRIDE

The beach is bare,
The tide is beckoning,
And dawn is breaking.

Still dressed in bridal gown,
I stare out to sea and savour the pain,
Of wounded pride and public shame.

I wonder where my groom is now,
Why he left me,
Did he not love me?

Discarding my earthly possessions,
The tears stream down my face,
And I welcome the sea's cold embrace.

Matilda Radcliffe (14)
James Allen's Girls' School

SWEET POISON

Spun gold hair
And pure was her skin.
Fine artistic hands
And posing, smiling lips.
Like the love goddess, Venus.
Now different in such venomous ways.
Hawk bred eyes: sharp as a spinning needle.
Cruel, cruel like an unloved pet.
A rosebud: sweet smelling, delicate
Hiding its bitter black thorns.
She was sweet poison to me.

Eleanor Harris (12)
James Allen's Girls' School

SOMEWHERE

Somewhere in a field,
Far away from here,
A black horse stands,
Next to a massive
Chestnut mare.

They stand grooming
Each other
Happily,
With not a care in the world.

Suddenly their heads fly up,
There is a thundering of hooves,
They have moved away
From each other,
To get some peace and quiet.

The same black gelding,
Now stands grazing on his own,
His mane and tail flowing in the wind,
And his blue eyes sparkling,
The gentleness in him shining out.

Gemma Gaitskell-Phillips (12)
James Allen's Girls' School

IN YOUR SHADOW

I sink in thoughts of yesterday,
When you knew how to get your way.
You whispered fairytales I longed to hear,
As I lapped them up you drew me near.
You saw your chance and soaked me through,
Learning from my mistakes I failed to do.
Again my reality you smoothly stole,
My defences dissolved and you took control.

Now haunting dreams swim in the air,
Through melting eyes I wish you cared.
Your phantom is slowly drowning me,
In your perfect idealistic sea.
Floating in your inanimate lies,
Waiting patiently for them to die.
Still silently your image washes inside,
And your shadow is still alive.

Nina Wafula (14)
James Allen's Girls' School

FRIENDS

Hurt, worried, mixed up inside
I just can't work out why she lied.
Doesn't she like me anymore?
A smile on the outside but my heart is sore.
My best friend is gone, she was all I had,
Now all her friends just think I'm sad.
I always say hi, but she just walks past,
I wonder how they turned her against me so fast.
If I call she'll be out with new friends
She never replies to the letters I send.
I long to go out, we'd have so much fun
But when I approach her she just lies and runs.
I think of the way that we used to be,
I never thought she'd turn against me.
But now I am done with trying to mend,
I know what it is to have a true friend.

Lucy Taylor (12)
James Allen's Girls' School

WILLOW

The weeping willow is a dancing lady
Swaying her arms so magically
But the winter comes and tears her green gown
She weeps away tragically

The weeping willow is a dancing lady
Drifting lazily in spring
Her misty eyes are happy, with what
The season will bring

Her emerald green, wispy long hair
Sweeps across her face
Runs down her back where her slender
Figure is patterned with brown lace

The autumn comes and she goes to her best
Dancing to her songs
Her gown has changed, her dress is different
From green to gold and bronze

The dancing lady has come to a rest
For now the winter is here
she shall dance no more in her gown of splendour
Her eyes roll away a tear.

Shreya Raghuvanshi (11)
James Allen's Girls' School

PICASSO

Picasso paints, Picasso draws,
Picasso sculpts different flaws.

The nose is green, the eyes are square,
It's something from your worst nightmare.

Though born in Spain he lived in France,
His art was different and advanced.

I'm not Picasso's biggest fan,
Because he is a mixed-up man.

Jessica Clark (11)
James Allen's Girls' School

LUNCH TIME

The town gossip pigeon,
Who can never seem to match her clothes
Or keep her wig pinned in the right place,
Is having tea and scones at the café
Muttering to herself.

Further down the street
The housewife bluetit
Just rushed out of her house,
With her apron still on,
To the grocers, because
She ran out of fishfingers for tea.

At the restaurant,
The well-trimmed business duck
Is discussing business prospects
With his colleagues, on a lunch break.

But now it is two-thirty
And lunch is finished
And everyone in the town
Returns to normal.

Nneoma Ulu (13)
James Allen's Girls' School

THE TIGRESS

Her eyes as bright as fire.
Her teeth are as white as white can be.
Except the faint blood stains on the
End of her canine teeth.

Her short soft teddy bear-like fur
Pushed past the tropical leaves,
Which hid her in her prime.
Her paws cautiously padding the ground
As though she was ready to pounce.
There was a deer on the other side of the tree.
Suddenly the tigress pounced,
With one great swish she cut the deer's throat,
And fed her three young cubs.

Stefanie Menashe (11)
James Allen's Girls' School

SWIMMING

I stretch out forward into the air
My feet push off without a care,
I spring right up into the sky
And stretch myself so very high.

Into the deep blue water I go
Hoping that I'm not too slow,
I reach out forward and then pull back
Now I think I have the knack.

Down the lane I go quite fast
Trying not to be the last,
I'm near the end, I haven't long
Now I know the race is on.

Emma Findlay (11)
James Allen's Girls' School

Death And Squalor

The black rivers of death flood over so many,
They spread and flow,
And make more tragedy
In so many people's lives.

Squalor and lack of hygiene,
Hardly any room to move,
Screaming and crying,
Shouting and sobbing,
This is the life of some.

We sit at home on winter nights,
Drinking steaming mugs of tea,
Snug and cosy, warm and happy,
Then going to soft fluffy beds.

In countries far and even near,
People freeze to death.
They know no better
Than their simple sad lives,
And some don't even care.

Claire Willman (11)
James Allen's Girls' School

Night

Darkness is the key to the unopened door of expression.
I unfortunately hold this key firm in the palm of my hand
In the fortress of my mind my recollections endeavour
Guiding the way for my thoughts to follow.

Katie Harney (14)
James Allen's Girls' School

The Sun

The sun is big and burning bright,
Pushing the clouds away with all its might,
Silently it moves from east to west,
Whilst some of us are wearing woolly vests!

We all have our own opinions,
But mine is that:
The sun is there burning away,
Thinking how hot it is today,
Imagine all that hard work,
When at the end we just smirk.

It's time for the sun to say goodnight,
And the moon to move in,
Whilst we all close the lids on our bins,
Good night mister sun!

Nadia Elsadani (11)
James Allen's Girls' School

Wet Sand

As the waves greet the rocks,
The gulls are having a gossip.
As the crabs race on the shore,
The thunder is giving a warning.
As the raindrops hurtle down,
The hope for the new day's shattered.
As the rain stops and the sun comes out,
The laughter of the sun is felt.
As a man walks across the sand,
He stops, looks around him and says
'Oh, what a joy it is to have wet sand between my toes!'

Omolola Akitoye (13)
James Allen's Girls' School

THE LADY OF COLOURS

The lady of colours,
With her dress so bright,
Is going to give us,
A wonderful night,
With velvet dark blue,
And moonbeam so bright,
It's going to be a wonderful night.

The morning will come,
With a yawn from the sun,
And if it will rain,
A rainbow will come,
With countless colours,
So wonderfully bright,
All thanks to the lady of colours.

Federica Amati (11)
James Allen's Girls' School

SLEEP

Drip . . . drip . . . drip . . . drip.
The tap in the corner is sending me to sleep,
like a hypnotist.
My eyelids are falling . . . falling . . . falling.
But no, I'm just too hot.
I can't open the window or the door will creak.
No position is comfortable,
maybe if I lie like this,
going . . . going . . . going.
Now the baby next door is crying.
Ah quiet!
It is so extraordinarily, difficult to . . . get . . . to . . .

Eleanor Simon (13)
James Allen's Girls' School

CRYSTAL WATERS

In the calm ocean waves
Underneath the stars
A figure appears
During the midnight hour.

A woman with pale blue skin
And dark green hair
Only one ragged dress
Does she wear.

At night she walks
The long white beach
Shining so beautifully
That the ocean weeps.

When dawn breaks
And lights up the land
All that is left of her
Are her footprints in the sand.

Francesca Sidhu (11)
James Allen's Girls' School

AN OBSCURE IMAGE

This is the first time this has happened
In seventeen, eighteen years.
A strange, unseen, unknown face
In my mind appears,
On the window of my eyes,
A shadow lingers - he's in disguise.
On the door of my heart
Someone knocks, then disappears.

I feel his deep, hypnotic eyes,
Staring at me in scrutiny.
A vague face forms in the palms of my hands,
I ask myself, 'Who is he?'
The scent of his hands - still in my hair,
I call out to him, 'Are you there?'
No answer. But I feel his soft breath
Becoming distant. Is he leaving me?

Shalini Anand (15)
James Allen's Girls' School

LOST

Why's it always me that's late?
I'm looking for this thing, room eight!
I know it's somewhere round about here.
It can't just disappear.

Room one, room two,
I thought this was something I knew!
Up the stairs, past the 'No Entry' door,
Room three, room four,
There can't be that much more!
Round the mound of lost property: an old shoe,
                and a rejected locker key!
Room five, room six.
Oh no, if it isn't dreaded Mr Hicks!
Past the office, past the staff room,
Ah ha, there's the last room!
Room seven, room eight,
At last.
(Just a few minutes late.)

Kate Macrae (11)
James Allen's Girls' School

Through The Eye

The eye feels, the eye sees,
It picks up the joy, the sadness,
The deep depression,
It picks up the glint, the beauty, the delicacy
Of soft velvet,
The eye can feel the tears pour down the swollen
Cheeks,
The deep colours of the vibrant blue sea and the glistening yellow of
Crisp golden rays,
The deep dimension of the eyes can see it all,
The ecstasy, the eye can sense,
Through the vivid thoughts and imagination,
The piercing eyes, the innocent eyes, the defenceless eyes, the eyes of
Blossoming talent, the eyes of happiness, tranquillity, contentment.

Alice Philipson (11)
James Allen's Girls' School

The Sun

The moon's brightness was starting to fade,
When like a sleeping cat the sun began to uncurl.
It seemed to stretch its enormous whiskers before it started to grow.
It grew and grew until the whole sky was filled with light.
When the birds began to sing it seemed to smile with warm happiness.
The heat became more blistering and started to glow brighter
and more luminous.
Every living thing was shielding its eyes and waiting for the dazzling
heat to stop.
But it kept getting more brilliant.
Then gradually, slowly, it began to cool.
The sun began to drop and the air became calm and no longer bracing
As the sun sank and the moon rose in a wonderful exchange.

Natasha Evans (11)
James Allen's Girls' School

The Empty Playground

The squeaky playground gate swung slowly shut
As the last pupil trudged down the long, lonely road.

A punctured football sits flatly behind the old black dustbin
Its playing days are over.

The dark, stained buildings stare coldly down on the deserted playground
Their corridors silent, the classrooms bare.

A solitary squirrel hops onto the mossy bench
And crouches there, idly munching a chestnut.

The autumnal leaves are blown across the misty tarmac
To a heap in the corner. No children to disturb them.

Echoes of children's laughter are lost forever . . .

Rosalind Pedder (12)
James Allen's Girls' School

The Summer's Over Now

The summer's over now,
Those lovely evenings in the garden,
And picnics in the wood.
The bright flowers, orange and blue,
Are now overtaken by the morning dew,
I remember the days sitting in the sun,
When the summer had only begun.
But come to think of it I know it's all right,
It'll come again next year.

Emily Ashworth (11)
James Allen's Girls' School

THE NEW GIRL

She stands alone in the corner,
No one dares to talk to her or touch her.
The other girls pair up and snigger,
Whilst she stands, dumbly twiddling her thumbs.

The bell rings, everybody moves,
She gathers her books and runs.
Everybody disappears into silence.

The lone soul walks in one direction,
Lost. She walks the other way,
Lost.

She trembles as she runs to somewhere,
Somewhere new, somewhere strange.
She asks someone who tells her the way.
'Many thanks,' she calls as she runs.

She arrives at last,
Breathless and tearful.
People stare and laugh,
She mutters her apologies with a quivering voice.
Then she scuffs back to her rightful place,
At the back of the class.

Stephanie Burton (11)
James Allen's Girls' School

SECRETS

My soul is dying.
I'm trying to understand.
Can't you see I'm crying?
Why didn't you catch my falling star?
Maybe I wished our love apart.

I heard her face was as white as rain,
Smooth as the silk on her underwear.
He keeps her picture in a frame,
And when he sleeps he calls her name.

I wonder if she makes him smile
The way he used to smile at me.
I hope she doesn't make him laugh,
Because his laugh belongs to me.

Sophie Willmington (14)
James Allen's Girls' School

ANGELS

They fly around on silver wings
And everyone is happy when one sings.
They watch over us when we're asleep
And cheer us up when we cry or weep.
Smiling faces, dancing eyes
Not one feature to despise.
Never scornful or deceiving.
Always giving, rarely receiving.
Angels' smiles can be seen
Laughter can be heard
And love can be felt within.

Chloe Palmer (12)
James Allen's Girls' School

UNITED FANATIC

Submerged in a blanket of red and black,
The faces on your walls constantly gaze back,
Does BSkyB succeed? Will Martin Edwards relent?
Putting up with Ferguson's irritating accent!

Posh Spice revealing a bun in the oven,
Roy Keane is faced with a team to govern.
As Johnson gets injured, his teeth are clenched,
Surprisingly Sheringham and Cole get benched!

Blomqvist, Stam and Yorke are left with a task,
To accomplish every goal 'The Gaffer' should ask.
We won 4-1 on Wednesday and 2-0 today,
But next it's Arsenal, Liverpool and Barcelona (away)!

Chioma Onwubalili (12)
James Allen's Girls' School

MONEY

Money takes over everyone's lives,
If we didn't have any we might not survive.
It makes you greedy, it makes you mad,
And even so it makes you sad.

People say that money is a pain,
When the bills come they go insane.
But suppose when they said this they won fifty pounds,
They would sing and dance and jump around.

Money has its ups and money has its downs,
On many people's faces it puts a melancholy frown.
Money is a nuisance all in all,
If you ask me we shouldn't have the stuff at all.

Beatrice Smith (12)
James Allen's Girls' School

GUILT

Guilt,
It hangs over you like a black cloud,
Crushing and leading your mind,
Dominating your thoughts,

You can't escape it . . .

It crawls over you at night,
And disturbs you during the day,
It's always there,
Controlling,

You can't escape it . . .

When you least expect it,
You'll remember,
Then guilt crawls up your spine,
And pierces your mind again,

You can't escape it . . .

It builds up on you,
Like a ton of bricks,
But now the weight is too much to bear,
You held it in,
   But this time,
     This time,
        This time you just couldn't . . .

Alice Michell (12)
James Allen's Girls' School

THE CLOWN

The audience laugh as he struts around
In shoes ten sizes too big,
But a clown is an actor and a good one too
And shows no fear to me or to you.
No one notices the sadness in his eyes
But under all the make-up he softly cries.
Most people assume clowns are always jolly,
As one hits the other with his polka dot brolly.
He stands there laughing in the middle of the stage,
But really represents an animal in a cage.
After all his funny acts still no one wants to be his friend,
Without someone to laugh with, his sadness never ends.
When the show is over and the audience has gone,
The smile fades from his face yet no one asks him what is wrong.
He sits there all alone now, but there's always room for hope,
Perhaps he'll make a friend tomorrow,
Or will people still see him as a joke.

Alex Wigley (13)
James Allen's Girls' School

WATER LILIES

It's a blurred image
Of a lake in the garden,
Lilies red and pink
Blossoming on the green wide lily pads.
Reflections of a willow tree,
Brown and green
With leaves falling.

It's as if there were frogs
Watching the calm moving water,
Which flows with purple, blue
And yellow streams.
All this seen
From a large oriental bridge,
Amazing what the eyes can see.

Camellia Makhzoumi (12)
James Allen's Girls' School

AMELIA

Two strong callused feet, crooked toes and solid ankles,
one leg straight, standing like a pillar,
the other bent and resting on a chair.
A huge crumpled black skirt,
overshadows the peeping white petticoat.
A white bow secures the apron,
crossed at the back over a primrose blouse.
Resting from her chores,
she leans out of a plain opening -
a window but without the panes.
Amelia watches a woman across the street,
pinning up laundry and her hair,
shouting in her husky voice at an insolent husband,
as she stands on the balcony, drenching coloured plants.
Amelia listens silently as wisps of thick black hair
slip from her bun and fall round her face.
Sighing she closes the shutters, turns, and glimpses a crimson hibiscus.
Plucking it gently from the terracotta pot,
she places it carefully in her hair.

Laura Hooper (14)
James Allen's Girls' School

SUMMER

The sun lazily smiles,
Down on the restless sea,
And on the sunbathers stretched out beside it,
One of them, is me.
Children are playing,
Happily in the warmth of the summer sun.
Leaving little footprints
In the sand.
The sandcastles
They have left
Will soon be gone,
But the sun's memory of them
Will linger on.

Alanna Barber (11)
James Allen's Girls' School

THE GARDEN

The garden lies in shambles,
Full of nettles and brambles,
With ripe blackberries to pick in the summer
The redbrick path that leads to nowhere,
The broken earth that lies beside it,
The ashes from the bushes we have burned
The broken bird bath,
Covered in ivy and left to crumble.
The pots without plants that seem to belong there;
The old green wheelbarrow turned over left to rust.
Sticks of rotting wood to hold the fence up,
The weeds that strangle roses,
And then I turn my back
On the garden.

Isabel Jarrett (12)
James Allen's Girls' School

THE CIRCUS

The ringmaster in his smart clothes, shouts,
'Please welcome the clowns,' and they come out
In silly clothes and enormous hats,
One is thin and one is fat.

They do silly tricks and fall,
The audience, they cheer and call.
The clowns squirt water at the crowd,
And blow their trumpets very loud.

Now for the trapeze artists' turn,
To show their skills, for us to learn.
As they glide from swing to swing,
They twist and turn from ring to ring.

The lions are next, they look so wild,
Enough to frighten any child.
The lion-tamer, so bold and brave,
Faces the lions, he looks quite grave.

The magician, full of mystery,
Displays his magic for all to see.
They're hypnotised by his clever tricks,
As he waves his magic stick.

The elephants walk into the ring,
The sight of them is a sad thing.
As they balance on a chair,
Maybe wishing they weren't there.

The circus ends, it's time to go,
The ending of another show.
The empty ring, where it's all been,
Reminds us of the things we've seen.

Laura Tucker (12)
James Allen's Girls' School

MISSING YOU

To be able to feel,
The touch of your skin,
Like a soft sheet covering your soul.
Smell your hair,
Its freshly washed scent,
As it tumbles free.
To see your face, your eyes, your mouth,
Breaking into a smile, eyes sparkling brightly,
Happiness trapped within you.
Then,
I believed in forever.

Snatched away,
Before I was ready to give you up.
All I have left is memories.
Anything I would give to just share one more moment with you.

As I walk around the house,
Everything reminds me of you.
All I am left with is the hope,
That a piece of your hair rests between the pages of a book.
A flake of your skin lies between the covers of our bed,
The bed where I spent so many nights, missing you.

Katsura Leslie (14)
James Allen's Girls' School

THE HUNTER

His uneven stripes, like a badly papered wall,
Camouflage him in the dead, brown grass,
Only his huge, golden eyes are visible,
Looking like two new coins hovering in the grass,
He watches and waits.

The brilliant sun makes the lake look like a mirror,
Reflecting the lean figures of a dozen deer,
Standing by the waterside drinking the cool water,
All except one, standing away from the others,
She is the one he chooses.

Francesca Tyler (12)
James Allen's Girls' School

HOMELESS

The world is full of homeless ones,
Begging for some change,
Stripped of all possessions,
Black bags do not seem strange.

Their voices are so powerless,
To fight the battle fair,
Their hearts are empty and disturbed
'Why doesn't anyone care?'

Sleeping on the pavement,
Ignored by passers-by,
Sadly staring into space,
Wondering, 'Why, oh why!'

Life has been so cruel to them,
They deserve another chance,
The simple pleasure of a home,
Would make them want to dance.

A home is not a privilege,
It should be just a right,
Why should they have to be like this?
We *must* fight with all our might!

Lia Deraniyagala (12)
James Allen's Girls' School

AGORAPHOBIA

The clock struck twelve, it was time to go home,
Five minutes' walk in a dark street, all alone.
Every day I dread this, but more so today,
There's something lurking behind me,
Something black or grey.

Two more streets to walk through,
But I could bear it no more,
This thing kept on following me, it was impossible to ignore.
I'll start to change my pace, just slightly quicker,
But this thing seemed to be just as near, if not even nearer.

By now my walk had turned into a fast run,
My heart was beating louder, tum, tum, tum.
But I dare not look back, no,
The thing seemed to be running as well,
Every action I made it copied, without turning, I still could tell.

My whole body was now shaking,
Not from coldness, but from anxiousness and fright,
As I tried to run quite unsuccessfully,
As there was neither help nor light,
But now, I was just seven metres away from home,
But it seemed so long, the street was empty -
Only the thing and I, alone.

I quickly opened the creaking gate,
And took out the silver keys,
I opened the door -
I could take it no more,
I was terrified and was about to freeze,
I rushed inside and slammed the door,
But there was something I could no longer see,
The things had disappeared just like that.
But where had it gone?

Camilla Spoto (12)
James Allen's Girls' School

A Bird's Eye View

As I fly in and out the clouds, I spot the end of the
Great forest I was born in,
In the distance I can see two high sheer cliffs;
Next to the cliffs, two hills with fanatical walkers.
Two large farms lie back to back.

One solitary house stands a mile away,
From past experience I know the arcane house is full of rancour,
There is no sign of life anywhere near the house
Unlike the farm where ducks and hens flounder all day.

Hedges and fences separate the two farms
Keeping out unwanted presences.
I do not land because a man stands in a field all day
Not moving a muscle but waiting to shoot.

Beneath me is a yellow field full of corn,
The farmer is collecting hay with his combine harvester
The hay to be made into a haystack that children will play on.
The farmer's wife is collecting the eggs from the hens.

Kate Stevinson (12)
James Allen's Girls' School

THE STAR OF LIFE

As it opens its eyes, the nations awake,
Not even a whisper does it make.
Silently it loiters here and there,
Giving life to everything, everywhere.

The auroral sky, like heaven it stands,
For us to admire all over the lands.
The birds twitter, the cocks crow,
Men and animals commence their show.

Beaming rays gliding over the land,
As light passes from water to sand.
Diffusing radiance, it stands up high,
As it enlightens the clear, blue sky.

The twilight zone beckons us all,
As night slowly begins to fall.
The cocks are silent, the birds nest,
Men and animals begin to rest.

Without this ever-glowing star,
No winter, no summer
No day or no night,
No life would exist without its light.

Shaista Mufti (12)
James Allen's Girls' School

PANSY'S LIFE

Growing up in a damp, dirty neighbourhood,
In a shady flat window,
No parents,
Being looked after by a lonely old woman.

Slowly she began to weaken,
Her blossomed body withered and stooped,
As winter came, she died,
And her seeds scattered for the next summer.

Nicola Roden (12)
James Allen's Girls' School

NIGHT IN A CASTLE

As I lie the embers flicker in the darkness,
The walls are so thick than you can hear nothing,
Not even the owls.
The cold stone flags was where I made my bed,
Listening, listening in the darkness.

Thinking of all the people feasting and dancing here,
The Lords, the children, the entertainers in this very hall.
It was a long time ago.
What interesting stories they would have told.
Now they are all dead and gone.

In the reflections of the fire I see my Game Boy briefly,
It looks so weird, so strange here.
It's all wrong.
The vacuum cleaner, the telephone,
They all look so out of place in this great hall.

Am I scared? Should I be scared?
All of the people who used to be here,
I don't know.
There's nothing here now though, is there?
So I don't think I should be scared.

Laura Parrish (11)
James Allen's Girls' School

The Harbour

The boat sat swaying gently,
In the warm afternoon breeze.
The sun glinted on the water,
As if sprinkled with gold.

A young boy with a net,
Wanders down the jetty.
He opens his hand,
And in the water he throws,
His only scraps of food.

A sudden eruption of fish
Circle around the pieces of stale bread,
Which float on the surface of the clear water.
A minute later the bread is devoured,
And all is still again.

Neusha Milanian (12)
James Allen's Girls' School

Nightfall

Night is drawing in,
I sit in bed with the covers up to my chin.
Gone is the day,
Here is the night,
The shadows fall,
Finishing the day, once and for all.
As I pull my covers tight,
Light is fading, day to night.
Lips silent, lying down, the day lost to sight.

Victoria Rolfe (11)
James Allen's Girls' School

THE HOUSE ON THE CORNER

The house on the corner stands alone,
Backed by the gloomy, grey skies
Once a thing of grandeur and impression,
Now a derelict and decaying slum.

Mud stains the cheaply whitewashed fence,
The gate has lost a hinge,
Weeds push through the cracks in the paving
And overgrown the untended garden.

The painted woodwork is peeling off,
The porch has a roof of cobwebs.
Accompanied by a musty smell,
Yesterday's milk bottles lie within.

The hitherto undisrupted calm is broken
As the door opens with a creak.
Dust motes dance in a ray of sunlight
Coming through a broken windowpane.

The walls are painted a stark white,
Damp shows through them too,
Where once there hung elaborate chandeliers,
An economy bulb flickers.

I step into the busy London street outside,
And look back upon the house
With a sense of depression and sorrow,
For it was once my childhood home.

Veronique Watt (13)
James Allen's Girls' School

SICKNESS

It's a cold, dark night,
With no one else in sight,
I feel so sick,
Better grab a bucket quick.

My head is burning,
And I'm tossing and turning,
A voice in my head,
Says get out of bed.

So off I go,
With my cute teddy in tow,
I'm so ill,
I'll take a couple of pills.

But they're so hard to swallow,
It will take 'til tomorrow,
I cough and I splutter,
My heart all-of-a-flutter.
Finally they're gone,
But still I hardly feel like singing a song.

I climb back into bed,
And all thoughts are gone,
I feel like I'm dying,
Please let me be wrong.

Morning has broken,
I wake with a start,
Oh cool, I can still hear my heart,
I rush like a fool,
To get ready for school,
I jump down the stairs,
Holding my shoes in the air.

Suddenly I sneeze,
And for a moment I freeze,
Oh blast, the sickness is back,
And it's on the attack.

Cassie Robertson (12)
James Allen's Girls' School

A DAY IN THE DESERT

The sun beating down on this desolate place,
Cacti spread for miles over the desert,
People and camels trying to survive,
The sand glowing in the heat of the day.

A cactus is standing curved and tall,
White spots at the bottom of the spikes,
The spikes sticking out to the corners of the earth,
Flowers popping up in designated places.

A camel walks along the sand,
Burning his hooves with every step,
His humps are high and round
His brown skin aching with the heat.

The wind has come again,
It is now freezing in the night air,
The people and camels are asleep,
But the cacti are in just the same places.

Kate Fletcher (12)
James Allen's Girls' School

VICTIM

She walked like us,
Talked like us,
And for a while, even became one of us,
But somewhere, deep inside,
I knew something was wrong.

She just didn't have a smile of joy,
She had a smile of fear,
So as I tried,
And as she cried,
She told me what went wrong.

She'd been bullied since primary school,
And now it's haunting her life,
She's desperate for a life to live,
For she's a lot of love to give,
Some with some help, and some care, she can do anything anywhere.

Denise Li (12)
James Allen's Girls' School

PARADISE

A ray of morning sunlight is distorted through lush young oaks
And glistens on the emerald garden below.
A blaze of violet pansies and a cloud of peach blossoms
Lay in a cluster unnoticed.
A soft breeze ruffles the frills on a sparrow's extravagant coat
As she glides deftly through the air.
A single crimson poppy grows proudly beside a worn gate
A scarlet beauty to all who beheld it.
The silent wilderness conceals itself in the depths of the hills
Paradise to all who come across it.

Nadia Huq (12)
James Allen's Girls' School

KILLER'S ANXIETY

The white corridors seem neverending,
The bright lights burn my head,
The blurs rush past, ignoring
My unanswered questions.
But I'm waiting.

In front, the blank wall is my companion,
It plays my reel of film.
Memories that are distant,
That almost was forgotten.
But I'm waiting.

Occupying your mind, while not knowing
What is to be known,
Is hard - I bite my lips.
Still the blood hasn't come out,
But I'm waiting.

There, there's the small girl, dressed as a fairy.
She cries, flickers and cries.
Then she skips down the hallway,
Giggles echo, kissed goodbye.
But I'm waiting.

Shadows gloom over me, I become dark.
Their expression tells me
The heavy cuffs scrape my wrists
I've known what was to be known.
And so I have waited.

Susan Mulanda Dale (13)
James Allen's Girls' School

SILHOUETTE

Stealthily, she climbed to the top of the hill
And watched the moon as it rose.
Even in the bright moonlight, she was black,
From her tail to her charcoal nose.

Nobody owns her, nobody feeds her,
Nobody beds her . . . and yet
She survives on her own, without a home,
She is nought but a thin silhouette.

She watched the world, approvingly,
With dark and lifeless eyes.
Never stirring, never sleeping,
Till the sun began to rise.

Nobody owns her, nobody feeds her,
Nobody beds her . . . and yet
She survives on her own, without a home,
She is nought but a thin silhouette.

When the town began to wake,
I dared to steal a glance
Up at the hill, to see if I
Could catch her, just by chance.

Nobody owns her, nobody feeds her,
Nobody beds her . . . and yet
She survives on her own, without a home.
She is nought but a thin silhouette.

But she is craftier than I
And, at the break of day,
With a last glance around, and a swish of her tail
She ups and sneaks away.

Nobody owns her, nobody feeds her,
Nobody beds her . . . and yet
She survives on her own, without a home.
She is nought but a thin silhouette.

Ali Paget (11)
James Allen's Girls' School

AUTUMN

The leaves have fallen from the trees and bushes,
All green and red and brown.
They fall so slowly, like the tiny, little snowflakes
Fall right from the grey sky!
And look, the birds are flying south!

Dirty, little sparrows paddle in the puddle
And people trying to get through the crowd,
Hurting each other with umbrellas.
The sun tries hard to get through the clouds,
But, no, the clouds just won't let
The sun get through.

The people rush and dash to get to school or work
And it's dark in the morning and it's dark in the evening
And there's hardly any light in the midday!
The cars just ignore the puddles,
And you just forget them too!

Natasha Rodionova (11)
James Allen's Girls' School

SENSES

You can't hear until you listen,
Listen to the birds humming.

You can't see until you look,
Look at the sun setting.

You can't smell until you sniff,
Sniff an early summer's breeze.

You can't taste until you swallow,
Swallow a soft scoop of strawberry ice-cream.

You can't touch until you feel,
Feel a rabbit's fur.

Stephanie Davies (11)
James Allen's Girls' School

LAKE

I see blue, gold and green
Stillness and calm
A fish jumps and falls,
Plop! back into the water
In the distance there are trees
Lush and quivering in the breeze.

I slip into coolness, breaking the calm
The water is silky and soft
I lie floating, looking up at the sky,
Unreal in its brightness.

A pair of dragonflies, their delicate wings fluttering
Dance for me, against a background of blue.

Niamh Riordan (11)
James Allen's Girls' School

A Mango's Life

I remember the days when I was young,
I hung from a mango tree and bathed in the sun.
Until one day a human came,
And from then on life was never the same.

I was picked off my branch on the mango tree,
Thrown in a basket with others like me.
It was then that my bumpy trip began,
On the bald head of a sweating man.

He walked for miles down a hot, dusty track,
I soon realised there was no way back.
He finally arrived at a quay by the sea,
It was the start of a very long journey for me.

The next thing I knew was a feeling unknown,
I was ever so cold but I wasn't alone.
Crammed into a box with a whole lot of others,
I'd never seen them before but they said they were my brothers.

We rode alone in the back of a truck,
There wasn't a roof (which was just my luck!)
The wind was cold and the rain it poured down,
I was somewhere in England - it was old London Town.

'Fresh mangoes, fresh mangoes, two for a pound,'
Voices were shouting, 'Yes please!' all around.
''Ere you go, darlin',' I was lifted in the air,
'This one's a beauty, I must declare.'

Thrown in a bag, it was stuffy and damp,
Jostled around, I began to get cramp,
Wrenched out of the bag and placed under the knife,
The end of my journey, the end of my life.

Laura Myers (13)
James Allen's Girls' School

ALL IN A NIGHT'S DREAM

As I walk, the wind whispers to me,
In a language only they can understand.
As I walk, the trees move towards me,
And then one puts out a hand.
A hand that's made from bark and tree,
That scares me through and through.
As I turn around to run,
There's nothing I can do!
The wood has now surrounded me,
And their gleaming eyes stare.
My heart starts beating faster,
As I look round in despair.
My legs are feeling weak,
As I fall to the ground.
When I come round again,
I hear a beeping sound.
I open my eyes slowly,
And in streamed all the light.
I looked around my bedroom,
And then I felt alright.

Shakia Stewart (11)
James Allen's Girls' School

SHALLOW

Silver nails, the latest clothes,
Parties, boys and fun.
You don't think what life's about,
This is all you've done.

Your life's just one big party,
Fun as this may be,
You've no idea what goes on,
You're too shallow to see.

A conversation with you,
Leaves much to desire,
As for your point of view,
There's nothing to admire.

You'll never stop your gossip,
So you'll never hear,
The sound the world is making,
Gently in your ear.

Penny Walsh (13)
James Allen's Girls' School

THE MORNING THAT WAS WEIRD

I'm half conscious when I get up,
My eyes are blurred.
I want to get up and then not.
The air is cold,
I have to in the end, so do.

It's summer but seems like winter.
I get up and,
There in front of me is a ghost.
It flew away,
I looked at the door to see;
That there it was.

I took a slow step to touch it.
My hand went through;
It suddenly leaped forward,
It was in me,
I realised it was my soul.

Suhanya Balasingham (13)
James Allen's Girls' School

My Message For You

Equality, fairness and no suffering,
Merely the few things I want.
But who will ever listen
To my cries of tear-fed want?

No fancy words can justify
The way that I do feel,
But if you tried for just a sec
You'll see that it is real.

Life is eternal and ours to rule,
But this cannot be fair,
That we kill others just for us,
And our selfish outer care.

I give this message, through a poem,
With nothing glitz or glam,
Simply to tell this life is ours,
To improve and not to damn.

Saba Khan (13)
James Allen's Girls' School

A Life Not For Me

I was walking home from school one day,
As I passed the mental hospital.
I looked through the barred up windows,
And I saw that it was very full.

Imagine what it must be like,
Confined to one tiny space.
Sitting there alone during the day,
And lying there all through the night.

Sometimes I see faces,
That look absolutely normal to me,
But inside, what must they be thinking?
Do they know that I can see?

Hopefully they are getting help,
Maybe they even know they are,
But whatever happens I'd like to think,
That their help will get them far.

Suha Shariff (13)
James Allen's Girls' School

THE LAST RIGHTS

Fine, grey hair strewn on the pillow.
Beads of sweat run down the shrivelled tired skin.
Her eyes have lost the spark, the pupil small.
Her hand in mine, limp, her long brittle nails
covered in paint chipped varnish.

She's staring right through me, a picture of a man
in uniform.
Outside the dawn is breaking, my eyelids feel
heavy, blurred.

Disinfectant fills my lungs.
My neck cricked against the itchy hospital
blankets.
It's noon, an untouched meal on the table.
A gilt frame stands empty, the photo in a clenched
hand.
Her hand is cold as stone, her lips are blue.
No breath passes through them, her body
completely lifeless.

Louise Dalton (13)
James Allen's Girls' School

MOUNTAINS

The moon and stars are rising
Over the pearly snow,
Everything is quiet
But not for long you know.

The silver of the moonshine
Rests on the untouched white,
The beauty of the mountains
Lasts only for the night.

The whistling of the wind
Is the only sound you hear,
No whirring of machinery
No sound upon your ear.

The sun has started to rise,
The silence to be broken,
There is movement on the mountains
For the skiers have awoken.

The lifts are moving all day
Everyone is in a rush,
Up and down the slopes they go,
But the snow is turning to slush.

Darkness is approaching,
Flakes are beginning to fall,
The mountains are deserted,
There is no life at all.

The moon and stars are rising
Over the pearly snow,
Everything is quiet
But not for long you know.

The silver of the moonshine
Rests on the untouched white,
The beauty of the mountains
Lasts only for the night!

Sarah Harper (13)
James Allen's Girls' School

THE WAYFARER

Clipping the boom onto the mast,
Pulling the sail in tight,
Undoing the reef knot on the moorings,
Sailing off into the deep blue.

Transferring the jib, rounding the corner,
Waving to the fish, straightening up,
Moving back on course,
Continuing the journey.

How peaceful leaning out,
Your head skimming the water,
Sitting back up again,
Feeling the cool water trickling down your front.

Feeling the wind in your hair,
Battering against your cheeks,
Hungrily filling the sail,
Going gradually faster.

Gliding along, going further and further,
Never looking back, never regretting a thing,
Seeing the sun just above the horizon,
Lost forever, only knowing this life exists.

Emily Willson (12)
James Allen's Girls' School

ANGEL IN SUDAN

No wings,
but watching still,
the solemn, silent lines of shuffling shadows
that wait for food and hope.
Mother and child:
eyes rimmed with flies;
tears like rain that never came;
bellies swollen with emptiness.

No wings,
but working still
to turn their darkness into light.
Going to fight all human greed,
war and waste and selfish ways.
Giving to meet their human need,
peace and quiet and loving hearts.

Amy Wynne-Jones (13)
James Allen's Girls' School

WILL I FIND THE ANSWER

No single matter on my mind,
Has left me with such doubt.
The tangled mess I've left behind,
Has left me feeling weakened.

No single matter on my mind,
Has so ever time-consuming been,
I've thought it through and through,
But still I found no solution.

So until I thought and could think no more,
I decided that I'd ask you.
In my mind my speech was printed,
I had reached that stage and then returned.

So here I lie, awake at night,
Wondering what you'd have said.
No single question has before,
Without an answer been so defying.

Susan El-Ghoraiby (13)
James Allen's Girls' School

PERSPECTIVE

Why are you there? Always beside me, always near me.
Why are you there? Calling my name, telling me to follow you.
I see you in the back of my mind, in front of me,
And when I sit alone I see only you surrounded by a lustrous light,
And when I weep I feel your warmth, your tenderness;
But I am not afraid.
You are my hope; you are my dreams,
You are my strength when *they* come and darkness falls.
You lead me away, away from *them* who are so pure, clean and white
And you take me to your hills, to the highest peak,
You tell me to jump - for I can fly,
And I do, my little golden unicorn, I do.
And as I fall down and down through a bottomless pit with the wind
                                       screeching haunting melodies,
I see you, my little golden unicorn, I see you smiling.

Phillipa Brothwood (13)
James Allen's Girls' School

BEFORE THE RED SHOES AFTER

You wear them down every day,
Sore and blistering skin.
Punishment for what?
They are the lowest of the low,
Dragging feet, alert mind.

Manic movement
Exhausting their victim,
Dragging body, alert feet.
Pounding muscles, screaming tendons,
Voluntary pain ripping and scratching.
Rest is magic,
Pain is magic,
Death, peaceful death.

Lizzie Sells (13)
James Allen's Girls' School

THE SIGHT OF A LIFETIME

In the middle of the oblivious African bush,
A small lonely tent stood in the dark.
Around the area snuffed a small, hungry aardvark,
While the gentle soothing wind rustled through the grass.

All of a sudden a pack of lions started roaring,
From the tent shone a bright beam of light
Ten pairs of annoyed red eyes shone back through the night,
But this did not deter the excited young man.

As the warm sun rose, the lions slowly moved away,
Leaving only a collection of fresh clear spore,
And a man fast asleep on a hard tent floor.

Victoria Mercey (13)
James Allen's Girls' School

TRYING

When I tried to tell you of the walls,
You shut me out,
When I tried to show you the poverty,
You had empty pockets and you
could not see me,
When I tried to step into the
warm light,
You left me in the dark, cold and hungry,
When I tried to reach for your hand,
You turned the other way,
Now I'm dead and buried,
You want to pay attention,
But you can help my people,
They are trying too.

Tara Brown (13)
James Allen's Girls' School

FORGET ME NOT

Forget the blue, angry face;
Forget the jealous, green body;

Keep the small, yellow,
dot of hope.

Which will grow to teach you;
Forget
Me
Not.

Jessica Bland (14)
James Allen's Girls' School

Summer Memories

Here is a little slice of heaven.
The sand stretches out for miles;
The sun bounces off the sea.
Seagulls swoop and cry - ah! Another tasty morsel.
Excited chatter of children,
Absorbed in a world of sandcastles and sea
And sandy sandwiches for tea.
The donkey plods his familiar route
His tiny burden dinging nervously above.
This magical paradise.

But now it is winter.
The sea is grey with breakers of white.
A few lone people walk the shore,
Huddled against the biting wind.
The children are no more.
But the seagulls swoop and cry.
'See you next summer -
See you in the sunshine.

Sophie Stanhope (13)
James Allen's Girls' School

Pressure

I see your eyes on mine,
Staring out with hope.
Looking for an answer
To why I'm on the dope.
I know how much you care,
It's just so hard to cope.
What I really want is
To tie my neck with rope.

Christina Stoneman (13)
James Allen's Girls' School

THE WORLD FULL OF FACES

The world is round and full of faces,
Global, strong and found in all remote places,
Lines of life, wisdom and pain,
Are discovered ingrained, creased and speckled on the rounds of faces.

Through the eyes you can explore,
All of the world's creations,
And see interpretations of land and sea,
That turn with the spinning universe.

The fragrance enters but never exits,
It smells spice and all things nice,
It's the nose that determines flowers in a field on a summer's day
From the smell of bonfires burning in autumn.

Anvils, stirrups and of course, how could I forget,
The hammers thumping away on the drum,
Hearing, in my mind is a mechanical engine,
Connecting a sound with a piece of your brain.

Mouths I might say myself are extremely important
Tastes the food from different cultures,
Feeds the body and gives us energy,
And enables us to live a life that we all deserve.

As you can see, smell, taste and hear,
Faces are as marvellous as the whole universe in one,
And many varieties of created faces,
But we all look similar to one another
But our features all differ from each other.

Chloé Beecham (13)
James Allen's Girls' School

FICTIONAL PARENTS

Don't you just hate your parents sometimes?
They make you really mad.
They nag, nag, nag all the time,
And tell me that I'm bad.

I try my best to please them,
In every possible way,
I try and try and try again,
But I end up in dismay.

I find them so exhaustingly sad,
They dress in awful gear,
Their clothes, so distinctive,
Which they dress in all year.

Grounded for no exact reason,
I feel like I'm stuck in a prison,
Hate my parents for being so cruel,
My anger has boiled and risen.

Embarrassed for being their daughter,
In words I cannot explain,
I feel I could curl up and hide,
I'm in pain, in pain, in pain!

Claudia Moselhi (13)
James Allen's Girls' School

The Life Outside

When I go outside
    I see trees that
Look really wild like
    Curly hair.
A blue background
    With clouds that
Spread out like candyfloss

I see grass as green
    As a coloured pencil
The grass feels moist
    Like a wet flannel
And smells really fresh
    Like a scented flower
The bark on a tree feels
    Really rough like
Sawdust but not as
    Solid as a rock.

Emma Cleary (12)
Kidbrooke School

Irresistible Chocolate

As you unravel the crisp silk wrapper
The smell hits you
That's when you know you want to indulge
In that thick, sweet, creamy irresistible bar,
And that is how I know it's chocolate.

Vimala Ramalingum (13)
Kidbrooke School

COLOUR POEM

I am the colour of a rose
Because I blush when someone says my name.
My colour is a sunny leaf,
I can feel the sun's rays on me.

I am the colour of shallow water,
Because I float all around the world.
My colour is the colour of wallpaper,
Because my life is stuck together.

I am not the colour of the stream
Because I am not sad with my life,

But my colour is a sunny sky,
Because I am happy with my life.

Thuan Ho (12)
Kidbrooke School

COLOUR POEM

I am the colour of a hurricane
Who takes things away
I am a water hog because
I rain all the time.
I am the colour of a school
Because I go there to learn.
Mr Fell is the colour of lightning
Because he gives people detention
When they are naughty.

Sumith Suri (11)
Kidbrooke School

Colour

I am the colour of dull
I am the colour of the deep sea
I am the colour of the chocolate sea
I am the colour of the muddy dirt
Because it's messy and yuck.

I am the colour of anger
I am the colour of the summer leaves
I am the colour of the strawberry leaves
I am the colour of sun
Because it's full of energy.

I am the colour of vanilla
I am the colour of sweet wine
I am the colour of the bright rose
I am the colour of the gleaming snow
Because it's pure and calm.

I am the colour of lightning
I am the colour of thunder
I am the colour of pouring rain
I am the colour of a hurricane
Because I'm fast and strong.

Arti Hirani (12)
Kidbrooke School

A Sunny Day

Some flowers look like bells or balloons
The trees feel like paper
The grass is sparkly and wet
The red tree looks like it is coming towards me.

Joanne Oringa (11)
Kidbrooke School

WHAT COLOUR AM I

What colour am I,
I will never know.

People say I am white,
I think they are not quite right.

Some think I am red,
Only when I don't get my Big Mac.

Lots say I am the colour of pink,
Yes right like I am the colour of a Barbie sink.

What colour am I,
I will never know.

Saulo R Moreira (12)
Kidbrooke School

I AM THE COLOUR OF

I am the colour of a teacher teaching,
Writing on the blackboard like a dashing star.
I am the colour of a human being walking
My footsteps near or far.
Mr Fell is the colour of chalk
Because he is full of English to blast out,
I am the colour of snow.
I am the colour of a burning flame.
I'm hot and spicy.
I am the colour of the sun,
I hope I shine so brightly.

Laura Cullen (11)
Kidbrooke School

Colour Poem

I am the colour of a midnight puddle,
I sparkle in the night,
I am the colour of a pale white ghost,
I give everyone a fright.

I am the colour of rushing waves,
I push everyone out of my way.
I am the colour of the bright sun,
I shine every day.

I am the colour of an oak tree in the spring,
I'm losing all my leaves.
I am the colour of a great big wood,
I'm as big and tall as the oak trees.

Faye Dar (11)
Kidbrooke School

Colour

I am the colour of lightning
Because I am so fast
And I was like it in the past.
I am the colour of a loaded gun,
Because nobody knows what I have done.
I'm always well dressed
Because I'm just the best.
I am the colour of a bee
Because I like to be free.
I am the colour of a basketball
Although I'm not tall.
I'm the colour of the sun
That's what says my mum!

Indika Maleuwe (12)
Kidbrooke School

Chocolate Poem

I love chocolate
Chocolate loves me
When I eat it
I am happy

Chocolate Galaxy
In my hand
Then the Maltesers
Made a band

Chocolate chocolate
In the shops
On the shelves
It makes me pop

Chocolate
Chocolate
It's
Lovely.

Ryan Hayes (13)
Kidbrooke School

Colour Poem

I am the colour of a bat flying at night
I am the colour of the sun because I am nearly always cheerful
I am the colour of the sky
I am the colour of leaves in autumn because
I get up angry in the mornings
I am the colour of the sea
I am the colour of Arsenal's football shirt
Because I am good at football.

Kira Etherington (11)
Kidbrooke School

MUD, LEAVES, GRASS AND CLOUDS

Trees have rough leaves
and a hard and crinkly trunk.

Grass is long and thin,
thin as paper. It smells of dew.

Roses are red as blood
or yellow as the sun.

Mud is as dark as an ape
which makes me faint.

The clouds in the air curl around
they look like candyfloss.

Satwant Bansal (11)
Kidbrooke School

CHOCOLATE

As it sits there laying
so lonely on the bare table
It beckons me as my hand
grabs the smooth tender surface.
As I slip my hand through the golden cape
the slow but pleasurable sound is like
music to my ears as the first piece is
tenderly placed on my tongue.
Slow melting hmmm
heaven.

Adam Fuller (13)
Kidbrooke School

GALAXY

Open the brown and golden wrapper.
When you peel back the wrapper
it sounds like you're turning
a stiff and crisp page in a book.
It feels smooth and melted.
I feel hungry and savoury and ravenous.
I am desperate.

Kerry Vincent (13)
Kidbrooke School

CHOCOLATE POEM

As I open the fridge
to see the attractive Wagon Wheel,
I pick it up and strip the wrapper off.
I take a chomp and see the lovely
marshmallow and biscuit.
It is very mellow and soft.

Lee Nicholls (13)
Kidbrooke School

GALAXY

Brown and gold
I listen to the bar
It sounds like the sea crashing
Saliva begins to rush to my mouth.
As I pick it up it smells like fresh chocolate
I think I'm in heaven as I bite into it.
As I finish it my memories of the bar
begin to go.

Simon Foley (13)
Kidbrooke School

My Colour Poem

I'm the colour of a red rose
because I smell fresh.

I'm the colour of cool tangy
Doritos because I am sweet and
crunchy and everybody loves me.

I'm the colour of the school
because everyone wants to be in
me to learn.

I'm the colour of the sun
because I am happy and cheerful
and everyone wants to see me.

I'm the colour of lightning because
everyone is scared of me.

I'm the colour of a poem because
I am funny and sweet and everyone
wants to read me.

I'm the colour of a heart because
I am red and shapely and good
for Valentines.

I'm the colour of Lisa from the Simpsons
because I am so brainy and great
at the trumpet.

Adelaide Mendy (11)
Kidbrooke School

RED HOT POKER

I saw a part of tree
It is like the letters of the alphabet.
A tree that is all red, orange and
        pink and looks like fire.
Some of the tree's branches are curly
        and wiggly they look like pasta.
The leaves on the trees are as thin
        as paper.
The trees are very tall and very small.

Sarah-Jane Bailey (11)
Kidbrooke School

EVERY PETAL

Every petal on a rose is the shape
Of a balloon,
The colours are as beautiful
As a rainbow high in the sky,
The smell fills the air with
The sweet scent of a peach fruit,
The colour of the bushes
Is green like lime
First picked from a tree,
The leaves are different shapes and sizes,
On every leaf there is a vein thin as string.

Lisa San (11)
Kidbrooke School

In The Garden

The roses have lots of thorns
and feel like a hedgehog.
Smells as sweet as fruit
and petals feel like velvet.
The dew on the grass is as sparkly
as a glass of lemonade.
The dew sparkles like stars on the grass
The house feels as rough as broken wood.

Anne Louch (11)
Kidbrooke School

Images

Dew on the grass sparkles like stars
Roses are as soft as velvet
They smell as sweet as fruit
The clouds are as soft as cotton wool
The sunset in the distance looks like water
Colours run together.

Angela Pearson (11)
Kidbrooke School

The Old Bench

The old bench is damp and rough
It is deeply marked,
Drawn on and scratched.
Its scratches
Are like the lines on your hand.

Nathaniel Gray (12)
Kidbrooke School

Outside

The bush is big and fluffy like a hamster
The sky it cloudy
With white misty clouds and they spread out like water
The window
Is dirty like a crocodile
The bench
Is old and is starting to go green like paint
The school
Looks very big like a great giant elephant
The fence
Is big and has lots of holes in it
Just like a rat has bitten lots of holes in it.

Matthew Baiden-Adams (12)
Kidbrooke School

As Sharp As Glass

The roses are rough yet as thin as a piece of paper
Different colours stand out clearly,
Sprinkled with tiny glistening drops of dew
On the inside of the roses, petals are surrounded by rough leaves.
They stand tall on a long stem
With thorns as sharp as glass, almost covering it.

The leaves of these trees have no scent,
They curl over like an empty snail shell.

Tamla Jane Hall (11)
Kidbrooke School

ANGRY AUTUMN

The dim glowing sun,
is hiding in the clouds.
The dark grey sky, as grey as a rock
shows angry storms are brewing.
Autumn leaves,
as brown as mud.
The strong blowing winds
whistling down the playground
with the speed of a tiger.
The green grass
is shivering in the wind.

Vinh San (12)
Kidbrooke School

SMELL, TOUCH AND FEEL

The grass smells fresh like fresh water
From a freshwater stream.

The roses are as rough as a leather jacket
But the petals are nice and smooth.

This tree is wrinkly like old skin,

And that's all I can see, smell, touch and feel.

Jenna Seymour (11)
Kidbrooke School

The Autumn Poem

The ivy looks like water
Coming over a mountain.
The tree's bark
Is rough, like a brick.
The dew on the grass
Sparkles like silver glitter in the sun
And the tree's branches
Look like pigtails
Blowing in the wind.

Reece Parkinson (11)
Kidbrooke School

A Delicate Poem

The long grass is twinkling in the wind
Beside the pink, delicate, thorny rose bushes
The brown trees with shiny, delicate leaves
Are as smooth as tissue
Hanging off twisted branches
Like raindrops
The roses are as delicate as paper.

Chrissy Sheridan (11)
Kidbrooke School

THE LIFE OUTSIDE

There is a little bush of roses
That smells of ice-cream,
There is a little tree that looks like pasta,
A tree has red leaves
Looks like a tree on fire,
Orange and yellow flowers look like thin balloons.

Claire Reader (11)
Kidbrooke School

SANTA CLAUS

Christmas is here and he travels the world
He'll go anywhere and even get you pearls
He'll give children anything they choose
But has to take a rest once in a while for a snooze

If you were naughty he'll leave you no toys
But if you're good he'll leave toys for girls and boys
He comes to your house once every year
Making sure the reindeer don't have any fear

He eats your mince pies and drinks your beer
Knowing the children are safe and near
Tip-toeing everywhere humming quietly ho, ho, ho
Laying one of the Teletubbies down named Po

He puts down a golden haired dolly
The last present he leaves is a teddy called Molly
Without a sound he leaves closing the doors
Who is he but our old pal Santa Claus.

Rachel Dunk (13)
Prendergast School

GREEN, WHITE AND GOLD

Green is the colour of grass
Green is the colour of a frog
Green is the colour of the forest
Green is the colour of shamrock.

White is the furry polar bear
White is the colour of my clean school shirt
Whiteness of the sparkles from the cold frosty snow
White is a soft fluffy cloud.

Gold is the colour of my new ring
Gold is the colour of the autumn
Gold is the colour of my friend's long hair
But all of these colours make up the Irish flag.

Tara Smyth (13)
Prendergast School

THE COLOURS OF JAMAICA

Green is the colour of the palm trees which sway in the sky's warm breeze.
Yellow is the colour of the sparkling crystal beach sand
Black is the name of a river that runs in Jamaica
Red is the colour of the costumes in the carnival parades
Blue is the colour of the warm clear sea
Purple is the colour of the moonlit sky.

Jamaica is made of many colours especially those that are bright
When you go there you'll know that I was right
Jamaica's a very beautiful place
Just looking around is sure to put a great big smile on your face.

Simone Peynado Clarke (13)
Prendergast School

THE MAD PROFESSOR

The mad professor has white scary hair
The mad professor has a big black chair
The mad professor has a big dark room
The mad professor sits with his scary hair
In his big black chair in his dark gloomy room

He wants to rule the world

He sits in his big black chair
He sits thinking what to wear
He looks in his wardrobe, it was bare
He sits and thinks I don't care what I wear

But he wants to rule the world

He makes his brew, thinking what to do
He thought of a plan which made a big bang
He looks outside into the world
Nothing happened as far as he could tell

Still he wants to rule the world

He jumps up and down
He goes mad with excitement
He watches through the window wide
And the world had turned fiery red

Great I can rule the world.

Claire Carbin (13)
Prendergast School

Autumn

   The leaves are red
        Golden and crispy
                The flowers have died
                        The grass is wispy.

Scurrying to and fro
To find something to eat
Squirrels are nut gathering
Before the long autumn sleep.

The wind all around
Is cold and sharp
The thought of winter
Brings pain to my heart.

Spring and summer
        Are both far away
                But the thought of them now
                        Helps us through the long autumn day.

Louise Smith (13)
Prendergast School

The Sea

In the blue, cold morning
The green sea is peaceful and calm
Ready for the rest of the bright clear day.

In the red, gold afternoon
The turquoise sea becomes upset
The dark waves grow disturbed and distressed.

In the angry, fiery evening
The sea is mad, the waves crash
Threateningly dark and evil.

But by the grey, misty dawn
The green sea is peaceful and calm
Ready for another blue cold morning.

Natisha Salih (13)
Prendergast School

NATURE'S THIRD DAUGHTER

Summer eagerly nudges her lazy sister to rise
Autumn awakes and begins to prepare
Her new three month home in the skies
Lying on a rain cloud, she tosses her hair, swivels around
And sighs.

With an elegant shrug of her shoulders, her heavy coat of crisp
brown leaves goes slithering to the floor
with a lingering shuddering sweep
Scattering auburn leaves everywhere in the little bounding leaps.

Autumn entertained by her friends in the sky
Rattles the trees with her gusts of laughter
But don't forget, when upset her tears of fury will drip
Through every roof and rafter.

Autumn casts her sultry eye over her solemn domain
A half sad smile, a last gust of wind, and a torrent of torrential rain
This is autumn's way of showing her satisfaction
At the completion of her three month reign.

Adele Scott (13)
Prendergast School

THE WATER BABIES

Tom was a chimney sweep
Who lived long ago,
Mr Grimes was the master,
Who was making him work through cold and snow,

He was just a small boy,
Without shoes on his feet,
If he didn't work hard enough,
Grimes made sure he was beat,

One day Tom saw a girl,
Clean and pretty, fast asleep on her bed,
He looked at his clothes all covered in soot,
The thought of escaping came into his head,

Across the fields and over the hills,
As fast as he could, Tom ran away,
To a cottage of a lady,
Who invited him in to stay,

He was fed, warm and dry,
All that night in her loft,
With the moon shining in,
The hay nice and soft.

When he went out walking the very next day,
In the countryside around,
He fell in a stream where he swam,
Like a fish, without making a sound.

He made friends with a salmon
On his way to the sea,
'You have gills now' he said
'Come along with me.'

They swam together, on to the sea,
Green and shadowy, deep and blue,
Where Tom joined the water babies
To live his life through.

Charlotte Macrae (13)
Prendergast School

WHERE DO WE GO WHEN WE DIE?

Where do we go when we die?
Is it that place we call heaven,
In that big blue sky,
Is that really where we go when we die?

Where do we go when we die?
Is it that place we call the cemetery,
Deep down in the ground six feet under,
I sit here and wonder,
Is that really where we go when we die?

Where do we go when we die?
Do our spirits go afloat,
On the blue river,
Sailing like a boat,
Is that really where we go when we die?

Where do we go when we die?
I can only sit here and wonder,
Why, where, how, who,
Has or hides the answer,
To where we really go when we die?

Natreema Kusi-Mensah (13)
Prendergast School

A Poem About Cats

Big and tubby, small or thin,
Cuddly and purring away at my feet.
Crouching carefully looking around,
Ready to run and hunt the birds.

Large green eyes and whiskers guide them,
Razor sharp nails and teeth protect them.
They love to chase long tails in a circle,
Sleeping a lot even more than me.

Going out at night looking for fun,
Seeking adventure and playful games.
When the sun comes up they return home,
Wanting their food, drink and a cuddle.

They miaow when hungry and purr with contentment,
Needing affection and plenty of attention.
In so many ways they are just like us,
Cats need love just as much as we do.

Karin Diamond (13)
Prendergast School

The Season Begins

The leaves start to gather,
Falling like dripping rain,
Crispy brown surrounds the earth,
Footsteps follow you hear crunch, crackle, crunch,

A breeze of cold winter is coming closer
Nearer and icy nearer.
Leaves are piling and flying,
As the wind is howling and blowing.

Trees are bare feeling threatened,
Brown fumes begin to appear,
Leaves are brushed from side to side,
Swaying along, forming paths.

Frost appears sticking to the ground,
Holding, gluing down the leaves as they appear.
I'm warm beside my burning fire,
It's the time and season to be at home.

Aysen Estref (13)
Prendergast School

THE SUN JOURNEY

The sun rose in the east,
Yellow rays of light
Shone across the fields
Clear and bright.

The clouds blew over
Covering the sun
Which had just appeared
So clear and bright.

With a puff of breeze,
The clouds were gone
Once more the light shone
Golden bright.

But now it's evening,
The sun rests and sets in the west
Leaving a rosy glow
In the sky.

Natasha Coleman (14)
Prendergast School

The Months Of Different Seasons

March, April and May,
This is when the flowers start to appear.
In a vast range of colours,
Red, orange and yellow.

June, July and August,
The flowers are blooming straight up,
The flowers are bright,
And the sun is high.

Now it's autumn and
Evenings are shorter and colder,
Sadly flowers are dying,
School is back once more.

In the last two months,
The bonfire comes, the bonfire goes
Christmas comes, Christmas goes,
Back to a New Year, full of surprises!

Nneka Carr (14)
Prendergast School

Diana

She was gone, she disappeared,
She was called the Queen of Hearts.
She was the first royal woman to touch
someone with AIDS.
She died, died in a car in Paris.
She was chased, chased to her death.
She was beautiful,
She was the English Rose,
She was Diana.

Sophie Bigmore (12)
Putney Park School

The Futility Of War

As the sun rises the light falls on a world full of death
Where every life is like a single breath.
So short-lived and no chance to survive,
These men have no choice and of their lives the are deprived.

Every space of ground is a grave,
But why should this be so when each of these men died so brave?
Why should their lives and the lives of their families be shattered,
And then forgotten as though they hadn't mattered?

And for what? A world at war with each other,
Every time one undeserving man is killed there will always be another.
This world where civilisation seems lost forever,
If war continues will never stay together.

Lucia Sabine (15)
Putney Park School

School's Out

S chool can be fun, but when that school bell rings,
C an't wait to get
H ome, down to my locker,
O ut of the door,
O nto the bus.
L et's hope I've not forgotten my homework again.
S chool's out, time for the PlayStation, time for games.

O h not forgetting homework to be done,
U nder my rubbish there's my desk to be found
T here I'll do my homework with my music on loud.

Elizabeth Carter (12)
Putney Park School

LIFE

Is a dream reality
Or is life a dream?

Are flowing tears, problems disappearing?

Are eyes meant to look in love
Or to stare in hate?

Is left handedness a sign of the devil?

Is fat a sign of spoilt
Or is thinness a sign of neglect?

Is life a fast flowing stream
Or is life a stationary wagon?

Is life like a game of kiss and chase,
Or of cops and robbers?

Life is a dartboard,
Sometimes you win and sometimes you lose.

Sarah Wheatley (15)
Putney Park School

MONDAY MORNING

Awakening by the dreaded noise of my clock
Feeling heavy as a rock.
Sluggishly I clamber out of bliss
(Oh why do I deserve torture like this?)
Into where doom now begins.
Monday morning what a bore
Five whole days of school once more.
Oh why can't I stay in bed and snore?

Penny Harland (16)
Putney Park School

The Sunken Graveyard

Ten fathoms deep beneath the waves
A sunken graveyard lies.
It tells a tale of battles fought and lost,
Now silently the war-torn wrecks
Have peeled their outer skin
And poison lies menacing within.
Slowly it begins to leak a black and deadly cloud,
Another battle shall begin
Upon the age-old sea.
This time no fierce or bloody fight
No crashing steel nor flames of fire
No quick or violent death.
Instead a blackness chokes
The beauty of the deep.

Elizabeth Straughan (15)
Putney Park School

My Horse

As we gallop through the fields,
Faster! Faster! Cries the rider.
Over hills and through the valleys,
Riding, alone, by myself.

On and on forever riding,
Fast as the wind through my hair.
Adrenaline making my body alive,
Soaring up, high into the air.

Then, winding down to a canter,
Slowing now, nearly there.
Then appears on the horizon,
Home is where I live; my heart is there.

Hannah Nurse (12)
Putney Park School

Sleeping Village

Red sun rising in the sky,
Sleeping village, cockerels cry,
Soft breeze blowing in the trees,
Peace of mind, feel at ease.
Early risers dogs and cats,
Roaming the streets,
Where people sat,
Resting their feet.
Smells of baking bread,
Drift over the air,
Heavy footsteps tread,
The morning beware.
Wisps of smoke,
Rise from chimney stacks,
Billowing fumes of coke,
Wind out of windows and cracks.
The early riser, pipe in hand,
Shuffles out to his chair,
Half buried in the sand,
And gives his dog a long hard stare.
Still peaceful, the village comes to life,
As the sun gains height,
Content the husband and wife,
Begin a new day in the increasing light.

Emma Hazou (15)
Putney Park School

THE DAY BEGINS

The dark, silent and sombre black of night,
Begins to lighten.
Deep blue gently sweeping into purple
The birth of day begins.
It feels like hours;
But only moments have passed.
A variety of day begins to appear.
The purple slowly changes into a maroon,
The colour of a deep red rose.
Then suddenly a brilliant orange takes over.
Don't blink or you'll miss it!
It's like a precession;
The minor colours pass first.
Then the almighty golden white of day appears,
The sounds of life begin,
Birds singing to the new day.
Flowers wake and raise their heads to the sun.
Soaking in its warmth.
Trees steam as the morning dew evaporates.
A cat stretches its body,
Yawning in the fresh, unspoilt air,
And walks somberously across the garden.
The humming of engines from night workers returning home
Can be heard in the background:
A beautiful, busy summer day begins.

Poppy Willcox (16)
Putney Park School

TEARS OF SORROW

I was silent,
Silent as a statue,
I didn't know what to do or say.

I felt hot tears welling up in my eyes,
I swallowed and blinked, and blinked again,
And the tears came rolling and crashed into my cheeks.

I then imagined what happened to my parents in the car,
So I tried to stop the tears from coming down,
But the more I tried to stop myself, the more my eyes got redder.

The veins in my eyes were like poisonous snakes,
Desperate to escape
To dry land.

They told me that I had to start packing my bags,
I didn't want to go anywhere,
I just wanted to lie down and let the other small part of my life
                              that was left, disappear.

Rana Haddad (13)
Putney Park School

CRYING

She felt tears coming on,
but knew she couldn't hold it in.

Any second it would come bursting out,
rolling, sliding off her tender mouth!

The anger that she felt on that day,
as she watched her baby fade away.

She knew it wouldn't be the same,
to hide the shame or hold her head high in fame.

The people would say 'It'll be OK'
but those lies just tore her apart.

She lay on her bed and said to herself
in an uncaring soft kind of way, 'I want to die!'

Elizabeth Shone (12)
Putney Park School

THE HORSE

There is no animal,
That shows such beauty and such grace
Whose muscles ripple as they move
That shows no hatred or anger,
But seeks love and friendship.
That does their very best for you
On days when it really matters,
That lets you take the reward
After a day's competition.
That relies on human care and assistance
When not in the wild.
That has allowed many wars to be won,
With such power yet so much obedience.
That comes in all shapes, colours and sizes
To suit all abilities and ages.
I am very proud to present this fine animal
As the horse.

Nina Thomas (15)
Putney Park School

DIVING

The waiting . . . anxious . . . ready to go,
The run up, the spring, the flight and so . . .
As we get prepared to dive off the board
And land in the water,
It's so important my technique doesn't falter.
One slip of the foot or wrong bend of the waist,
Oh dear! I'd better not be in too much haste.
Perhaps diving isn't so much fun,
I might have been better off going for a run.
As I peer down at the water below,
Perhaps it won't be so bad if I dive really slow.
I close my eyes and count to three,
Yes! I did it, I dived and felt so free
Like a bird in flight I spread my wings
I'm not afraid any more of doing these things.

Chloé Bellas (12)
Putney Park School

CAT

The small black purr . . . fectly shaped silhouette of the cat,
Bounded across the garden, leapt up on the wall and there she sat.

She sat on the wall waiting, in readiness to pounce
On a small unsuspecting creature, possibly a mouse.

She struts around the garden, with her black tail flicking high
Or stalking through the undergrowth with a highly inquisitive eye.

She always likes to be busy, she never knows what to be at,
Except of course when she's sleeping, after all she is a cat.

Lindsay Garland (15)
Putney Park School

CHERRY

Through the darkness we canter around,
the sound of Cherry's hooves echo on the ground.
'Faster faster' says the rider,
we come to the river glistening white
there is no bridge, what a fright!
As we defy gravity over the river high
the horizon seems to die.
We weave a beautiful pattern in the trees
the oak branches clawing against my face
but I do not care, I want to race.
Nearly there the ride soon ends
a chill of relief goes through me
it is not the ride, it is my horse, Cherry.
In the dead silence of the night
the fear ends in the stable's light.

Nicola Vasey (12)
Putney Park School

THE UNKNOWN

As I lie on the golden dunes and absorb the rays of heat,
I watch crashing waves rebound in the caves
While the sun beats down on me.

I begin to rise and drag my feet
Till I reach the edge of the beach,
I look behind and see no trace as the sand covers my feet.

I enter the calm glittering sea
And wonder how I can sustain its strength,
As it is much greater than me.

I dive down below to the coral reef
And think how I can possibly believe
That the beauty of the sea is so close to me.

While I am in another world
I touch the pearl of my dreams
And realise nothing is ever as it seems.

The emotions I am feeling
The sea is slowly healing
As I begin to discover my inner being.

When I rise to the top I am dreaming
That the tranquillity of the sea I am leaving
Will stay with me for eternity.

Camilla Hayes (15)
Putney Park School

DO I DESERVE THIS?

Do I deserve this?
To be locked up like I have no rights,
Lately we've been going one by one.
I know where they've been going.

I have seen my eggs go one by one,
To feed the humans' greedy appetite.
I have several chicks and I know,
That they will be gone within a year.

Why are we treated like this?
No one cares if we die or live.
We're just food for them!
I know my time has come.

I will be gone soon and I'll leave my chicks,
To satisfy somebody's appetite.
I have produced eggs to my heart's content.
I know I will be gone soon as I'm
The only one left in my cage.

I see row upon row of my kind,
I see the conveyor belt run under me.
I feel as though my lungs have stopped.
I know I won't see the light again
Ever, ever.

Emma Chapman (13)
Riverston School

Treasure For Pew

Pew is mean, old and blind.
He wants a chest
with treasures inside.
He was so mean one day,
his helpers left him alone
and ran away.

He stood on a road
helpless and blind.
What could he do?

A horse with its rider
came striding down
and ran over Pew.
He rolled into a ditch
bruised and kicked
and then he became stiff,
then he finally died.

Sunil Sonny (12)
Riverston School

I Am What I Am

I am what I am, and that be a pirate,
I am a heartless cut-throat,
I keelhaul people for the sheer fun of it,
And I plunder ships for their gold.
I feed people hemlock saying it's soup,
And that's what I am, a pirate.
Ay! Ay!

Richard Bond (13)
Riverston School

PIRATE POEM

Pirates are fierce and evil too,
They scare children,
So don't let them say '*Boo!*'
Some of them are blind, some of them are dumb,
Some are fierce, but most of them are scum.
The skull and crossbones is their flag, but
It reminds me of Blackbeard and Long John Silver.
They both are ugly hags.
Never get on a pirate ship for you don't know
What the pirates might do,
But what I know is that they are scoundrels
And so is old dead Pew.

Wing-Ho Tang (12)
Riverston School

PIRATE POEM

Ahoy! Matey as we sail the ocean blue
Join us on our journey as we quarrel, thieve
And search for riches.
Marooned we were, mutineers,
Killers and thieves we were.
We now live the lives of seafaring men,
As we stop at nothing to find our treasures,
And live our sailor lives.
When the time comes for Treasure Island
We will be rich, we will as our buccaneer
Days will be over and done away with.

Rian Butler (13)
Riverston School

PIRATE POEM

Pirate, pirate on the sea,
go to island, find treasure
Found the treasure they go 'Ha ha'

John Silver is the most evil
He tried to kill Jim and the captain
Jolly Roger in the sky.

Jim Hawkins is a little boy,
Met Ben Gunn in the deep green forest.
Tried to cut Hispaniòla adrift.

Wai Kit Lam (12)
Riverston School

PIRATE POEM

Singing on the branch above
I think it's just a little dove
But when I see a massive knife
I get a massive fright
Then the man wants a fight
So he drops from a great height
And oh what a dreadful sight
With a hat with scull and crossbones
And a voice with moans and groans
A black eye-patch
And a little backpack.

Benjamin Wilkinson (12)
Riverston School

NOBODY'S PERFECT

Nobody's perfect, not even a twin;
Their hair might be different,
or be less sparkling.
Their eyes are the same,
their nose and their mouth,
but nobody's perfect, not even a mouse!

Nobody's perfect, not even a mouse;
Their eyes might be bigger,
they might live in a house,
They might run and skip or be
caught by a cat,
but nobody's perfect, not even a rat!

Nobody's perfect, not even a rat;
They do not have wings or hair like a bat.
I can't think of anything else to write,
but remember, nothing's perfect.
not even a . . . kite . . . ?

Monique Grant (11)
Riverston School

THE GIRL I LOVE WITH ALL MY HEART

The girl I see here and there
mailing letters everywhere.
She mails some wrong,
she mails some right.
I love her with all my might.

Samed Aykac (12)
Riverston School

THE HILARIOUS THREE

Of all the classes it just had to be,
That of the hilarious three.
Alas I should have known;
That they're just a pain to my throne.
How unfair can this short life get.
I just want to hear about their death,
The hilarious three . . .
Then Fluke decided to visit me.
How this happened I'm yet to know,
But now, they've all joined the flow.

Olufemi Okulaja (11)
Riverston School

YOU AND ME!

When you love someone so deeply that they become your life,
It's easy to come to overwhelming fears inside.
Lonely I imagined I could keep you under glass.
Now I understand to hold you
I must open up my arms and hold you,
If you should return to me.
We truly were meant to be,
And I truly feel your heart will lead you back to me
Whenever you need me.

Rebecca Penfold (12)
Riverston School

LOVE

Love is something special,
You can't have it just like that.
You can't buy it or sell it,
Or magic it out of a hat.

Love is something special,
Love is like gold.
Love is something really good,
It's never new or old.

Love is something special
Love is really true
Love is something we all need
Love can leave us blue.

Maryanne Carlin (11)
Riverston School

HISPANIÒLA

H ere is a ship of great style
I   know it was run by
S ilver the one-legged
P irate and all his nasty seamen.
A nchorage where they stood
N ear Skeleton Island.
I   f they were going to find the treasure on the big island
O 'keelhauling I say
L egs of Silver and the
A rm of the leader of assizes will make my portion of the ò.

Niyi Falase (12)
Riverston School

OH WHY? OH WHY?
THE CRY OF BATTERY HENS

Oh why? Oh why?
Do I have to be here?
Oh why? Oh why?
I don't know,
I can never know
What layer I'm going to be
I just hate being a hen.

I hate the smell of other chickens' poo
that drops on my little head
Sometimes I feel like killing myself
but what on earth can I do now?
All the eggs that I lay
are taken from me
What have I done to deserve this?

All the eggs I have laid
could have hatched ages ago
and taken care of me.
With my beak cut,
how do I eat my food?
I always feel like pecking the farmer
but what on earth can I use for this?

Oh why? Oh why? Oh why?
After my friends have laid about 300 eggs
they are used for chicken soup.
Day after day, they go, one by one,
It's my turn to go now!

Daniel Olurin (14)
Riverston School

THE LAMENT OF THE BATTERY HEN

Why why why me?
I stink to high heaven,
I've got a hen upstairs who
keeps doing it on my head.
I wish she would stop it.

All my friends have gone,
and the love of my life was
slaughtered right in front of me.

This place has a sickly-sweet odour to it,
I wish I could escape.

Oh no I've done it again
my foot is caught in the cage.
I have barely enough room to breathe.

Lena Andreou (14)
Riverston School

MY LOVER

Once I saw a girl
I didn't know how to spell.
When she looked at me
her heart came to me until
she kissed me. When she saw me
she thought I was lonely.
When she kissed me
she thought I was honey.
When she kissed me again
she thought I was hunky.
Our love is one and only
so now we are not lonely.

Hurshal Patel (12)
Riverston School

WHO AM I?

I am a book
without a cover.
I am a friend
with not another.
I am a star
that cannot shine
I am a watch
that tells not time.
I am a letter
you forgot to send.
I am the heart
that no one can mend.
I am a parent
without a child.
I am the spice
that tastes mild.
My lip is a sham
That's who I am!

Pinkesh Patel (11)
Riverston School

THE MOON

The moon, the moon I wonder what it's like.
Cold and dark to give you a bit of a fright.
If I was on my own, I don't know what I'd do.
I suppose I would just have to find someone to talk to.
I would not wear a spacesuit, I'd feel too hot.
I would just wear normal clothes or maybe just a top.

Gemelle Canoville (13)
Riverston School

SCIENCE FICTION POEM

Flying through space,
watching planets fly by,
and without the wind in my face,
time sails by.

Watching stars burning billions of miles away,
the earth the size of a ping-pong ball,
and now I spend five days,
without a word of praise.

My foot digs into the moon,
I'm bouncing like a balloon,
the flag is forced in
and history has begun.

Nick Philp (13)
Riverston School

SPACE ABOVE AND BEYOND

Space, space, space
Far and beyond
Planets and systems aligned
Asteroids and meteors break away
Death of a star the birth of a system.

Beginning of a black hole
The explosion of a sun
In the blackness is undiscovered planets.

Michael John (13)
Riverston School

REFUGEES

The refugees come to our country
scared and frightened and wanting to hide.
They are shocked and scared of war
and want us to be on their side.
They are homeless with friends left behind
and only want us to be kind.

They have travelled many miles
but are glad to have survived.
They are fed up with running,
they all feel so tired.

Refugees are here, refugees are there,
Refugees are everywhere.

Lianne Hemblade (11)
Riverston School

REFUGEES

We came from a distant land
Where no one can understand
Who we are and what we do
And just where we are travelling to.

We are homeless, scared of war
We hear gunfire ever more,
Thankful that we got away
Hope now fills each passing day.

In our land was danger there
No food or shelter anywhere,
Now we live in a foreign city.
The past a memory, more's the pity.

Shaheen Ali (12)
Riverston School

THE GHOST CAT

Pussycat, pussycat, sitting on a ghost wall,
Pussycat, pussycat, miaowing until dawn.

Pussycat, pussycat, walking down the street,
Pussycat, pussycat, looking so neat.

Pussycat, pussycat, walking across the road,
Pussycat, pussycat, got run over and lay on the floor.

Pussycat, pussycat, how can I help?
Pussycat, pussycat, died right then.

Pussycat, pussycat, I will never forget you.
Pussycat, pussycat, you are no more.

Pussycat, pussycat, in the graveyard
Pussycat, pussycat, rises from the dead.

Pussycat, pussycat, is a ghost
Pussycat, pussycat, sitting on a ghost wall.

Nicola Watson (13)
Riverston School

I AM A REFUGEE

I am a refugee
I come from a country,
Where there is nothing but war.
I was terrified, I left my family
My school, and everything I care for.
I have no shelter, no money and no protection,
All my friends are gone.
I am tired.

Rolande Seudieu (10)
Riverston School

My Dream

My dream is to be a stuntman,
to be falling from 60ft high,
to be crashing into a brick wall,
to be parachuting down from the sky.
My dream is to be a stuntman,
to be breaking my legs and get hurt,
to be climbing trees and having fun,
to be rich and famous and hard.
My dream is to be a stuntman.
All my friends call me:

'Hey you, over there
what's it like to have no fear?
Is it cool? Is it fair?
I've seen more fear on a bear.'
That is my dream.

Chris Bancroft (12)
Riverston School

Refugees

A refugee from another country
Fleeing, scared of the war
Military occupation, running away
Glad to survive
Homeless, cold and hungry
Travelling all the time and shocked
No protection, no shelter
Sad to leave his friends behind.
Taking their pictures
To keep memories alive.

Michael Ehinmoro (12)
Riverston School

GIRLFRIEND

I looked in her eyes
and saw the skies.

We played in the sand
and she held my hand.

When we kissed
she made a hiss.

When we jumped
we made a thump.

Then the sand blew
away, and she went.

I didn't know where
she went.

Perhaps she went
with another guy.

When I see another girl
maybe there'll be love in my heart.

Scott Simpson (12)
Riverston School

REFUGEES

Refugees come from another country,
Refugees move from one country to another country.
Refugees have no shelter or protection,
Refugees never get much affection.
Refugees are always afraid of war.
Refugees must be shocked by what they saw.

Bilal Elahi (11)
Riverston School

THE PAID SPACEMAN

Everything is still
everything is quiet
the spacecraft is huge
everyone's having a riot.

On the moon
there's a smell of must
I've got the footprint
on the moon.
I'll stay here
and see you soon.

Time for me to go home
back to Rome
just another day
to get my pay.

Gavin Burton (13)
Riverston School

REFUGEE POEM

I am a refugee,
I come from another country.
I am a refugee.

I am tired, I am homeless, I am frightened
I feel hopeless, where am I?
Sometimes I want to hide.
And I feel glad I have survived.

I have left my friends,
My family, my photos and my memories.

I travel all the time
I never stand in line.

I am a refugee,
I come from another country.
I am a refugee.

Rochelle Edmondson (11)
Riverston School

MY POEM

I'm someone who comes from another country
May want to hide
      Who am I?

I have no shelter
And no protection
And I'm glad I have survived
      Who am I?

I'm homeless
Nowhere to go
I'm happy I escaped
      Who am I?

            I'm a refugee
            You know me!

Leon Powell (11)
Riverston School

MY POEM ON REFUGEES

There, there were the refugees.
Walking along sadly.
When they saw me they were shocked.
Scared and horrified.
He came over to me. I asked 'What's up?'
He said he was tired!
He said 'I come from Australia.'
I said 'You must be happy to have escaped the war.'
He said 'Yeah but I left my friends behind.'
I said 'You must be glad to have survived.'
I said 'Have you got any shelter or protection?'
He said 'No.'
I said 'Come round to my house.'
So we went home.
I asked 'Have you any family?'
He said 'No, they died in the war.
But I have some photographs on me!'
I said 'Who is that?'
He said 'That's my sister, she was shy!'
I said 'You must have some bad memories in your mind.'

Charantoor Singh (11)
Riverston School

LONG JOHN SILVER

Long John Silver,
Not a noble with no heart
The only thing
That kept him going
Was a bottle of rum

His brain was going
Tick tock tick tock
Like a clock
All through the day
With killing in his mind,
He was never kind.

James Martin (13)
Riverston School

THE CRUCIBLE

Tension is rising,
As the rumours are spread,
People are dying,
As the rumours get said.

Lying is not unusual,
Although it is a sin,
But the only way you can save yourself.
Is to make this terrible sin.

Revenge is sweet,
But is taken too far,
Many have died,
And now there's a scar.

A secret is difficult to keep,
If it is not truly white,
The truth soon be told
But will never be right.

People have fled,
People have lost,
Due to one girl,
A town pays the cost.

Esther Harrison (14)
Riverston School

REFUGEES

Someone who comes from another country,
Is sometimes called a refugee
He suffers much, so very much
You'll never want to suffer as much.

He's homeless, he's helpless
He longs for what is kind
He's very scared of wars
No one will talk to him at all.

And when he comes to think of food
He'll like to steal from other people,
For he will have no food to feed on
And then he will not like to starve.

Oh refugee! Oh refugee!
What shall the world think of thee?
Oh refugee! Oh refugee!
What shall God think about thee?

The scourge and sufferings shall
not be left unnoticed.
Mankind look the same,
But we think differently.

Shall this go unnoticed? - No.
Shall we lose love for the refugees? - No.
God created us alike
God bestows love on us alike
Please let us stop the sufferings of the refugees!

Tunde Dele-Ademola (11)
Riverston School

I Remember

I remember,
Her friendly reassuring smile as she answered the door,
And her sweet-smelling perfume that lingered for evermore.

I remember,
The way she would scrape back her wispy grey hair,
And tell me stories of her childhood, like she wished she was there.

I remember,
When she used to knit me clothes
And the smell of warm scones heating on the stove.

I remember,
Waiting anxiously for the news,
The doctor coming back
It's only now I realise what I have to lose.

Stacey Bogle (14)
Riverston School

Happiness Is A Sack Of Hay

The boy woke up on a midsummer's day
and knew that the time had come to be on his way.

The German army was coming very near
in his mind he felt great fear.

He packed his bag and said goodbye
he walked over the hill with a great big sigh.

It was a long walk to the sea
but eventually he was free.

He managed to get on a ship that was leaving that day
he spent his first night of freedom on a sack of hay.

James Allen-Thompson (11)
Riverston School

THE CRUCIBLE

Who treads so carefully at the dead of the night?
The wind blowing with all its might,
The leaves rustling in the willow trees
And the patter of feet
Who is it please?

Sylph-like figures dancing under the moon,
Holding hands and chanting to an eerie tune,
Their hair wild,
Their eyes glaring bright,
Scantily clothed, under the moonlight.

Mercy turns to the other three.
'Oh no,' she cries
'Someone is watching thee!'

They run dropping a dress on the ground,
Little do they know it will be found.
For their little escapade they think they will pay a price,
For not all the villagers are very nice.

As the story is told again and again
The lie becomes bigger
Causing much pain.
Witchcraft, witchcraft is the word of the day,
These foolish but innocent girls
Make the town pay.

Claire Pink (14)
Riverston School

WHY?

Why am I and the other chickens living like this?
We are cooped up in a cage no wider than A4 paper,
stacked row upon row of each other.
I am found by the south door,
I am in the ninth pen on the right-hand side
of the fifth row from the floor; and in that pen.
We are so tightly squashed that we excrete on each other,
which is not pleasant at all.
Our days are spent laying eggs for these greedy humans.
I stare outside and see the blue sky and the green fields,
I wish I could breathe the fresh air of outside.
I know I will die in six weeks which isn't long to go.
We chickens don't have a life - it's like our lives are made for humans.

Lanre Falase (14)
Riverston School

CEASED

Marooned on Treasure Island was I
The only personage on the island
Where I fell in to a swoon
I knew 'twill not be long till I cease.

Deeper in the swoon I fell
An amazing person about to cease
What was I to do?

Deeper still in the swoon I fell
Barely using my willpower to survive
And then I dropped
I had ceased.

Natasha Clarke (13)
Riverston School

Treasure Island Poem

The story 'Treasure Island' is about a little boy called Jim.
At the start of the story he works in his parents' inn.
Then he went as a cabin boy on the Hispaniola,
And met a famous pirate called Long John Silver.
Other pirates he happened to meet: Billy Bones, Black Dog Pew
And Ben Gunn who knows all about Flint.
Long John Silver is a mysterious character,
He cooks, has a parrot, kills and shoots,
But nobody knows what he's really up to.
Night and day he searches for treasure,
Will he get the gold pot or will he never?
And so the story does go on,
Will Long John Silver find the treasure, or will I be wrong?

Katie Firmin (12)
Riverston School

Stormy Night

Stormy night,
gives me a fright.
Thunder roaring,
rain pouring.
Leaves on trees rattling
coconuts falling to the ground
sounding like drums.
Louder louder louder!
Making me cry.
All my friends saying 'Tolu, dry your eye
at the end of the night,
it will be alright,
when the storm goes away,
the rain won't stay.'

Tolu Ogundipe (12)
St Saviour's and St Olave's School

What Are Little Brothers And Sisters Like?

What are little brothers and sisters like?
They kick and pull your hair.
You are pulled over here,
And you are pulled over there.
Then they have a little rest to get
Their energy back,
And while they are doing that you are thinking
Of a way to get your own back.
But what a stupid fool you are.
You know they always win.
So why not give up now?
And stick your head in a bin.
They run and jump and mess about,
And when you want to watch TV
They scream and shout.
So now the day is over,
At last they have gone to bed.
But I wouldn't be without them,
No matter what they've done or said.

Rebecca Reed (11)
St Saviour's and St Olave's School

I Want . . .

I want love, I want his love
I want that warm feeling
I want the butterflies in my stomach
I want Cupid's arrow to hit you and me
I want his smile to brighten up my day
I want to share good times with him
I want to see the sun rise and stars come out with him
I want him.

Ali Cairns (13)
St Saviour's and St Olave's School

Frozen In Time

She had a mind of a genius,
Did nothing wrong.
Hard to believe,
Quite old, but strong.

She had the qualities of a midwife,
Caring and kind.
No original background,
No secrets to find.

Dead as a doornail,
Lying on the floor.
Cold as ice,
Stuck to a brick wall.

Light as a feather,
Heavy as a weight.
When will she come?
No certain time or place.

Sweet as an angel,
Falling from grace.
Nowhere to go,
An enclosed space.

She was a song,
A sweet melody.
Just like the tides,
Of a drifting sea.

Omotola Awofidipe (13)
St Saviour's and St Olave's School

THANKS TO GOD

I thank you Lord that from above,
You send my family to bring me love,
They have so much love to give,
I'm so happy to live
I get happier every day,
So much happier in every way.

It was sad when my nan died,
I sat down all day and cried.
We give so much love
Sometimes I think I come from a dove.

When I die
I want to wear a bow tie,
Buried next to my dad and mum
With my dog and pedigree chum.

Kelly Fordree (12)
St Saviour's and St Olave's School

THE SEA POEM

Fierce and hungry, fierce and wild,
The sea monster has struck again,
In the cold winter's night.
It crashes with power against the rocky cliffs,
The roaring waves moan and cry as they hit
anything that is near them.
Then summer come and the waves are calm,
They blow lightly inviting people to come.
The sea monster goes on shore to get a sun tan,
But just you wait and see, just you wait for winter next year.

Seyi Omotayo (12)
St Saviour's and St Olave's School

AT WAR WITH THE SEA

The humans were no match for the deadly sea
They wanted to retreat
The sea wanted to fight
It was determined to eat them alive
And spit out their bones

One of them got free
But the sea overtowered him with its hands
And brought him back in.
Again and again the humans made their way to shore
But again and again the sea pulled them back in

It was like a fierce dragon pulling them in
And one by one taking their lives.
It was like a vampire in the night
Sucking out their blood

Oh great god of the sea
Why did you pluck out our eyes
For us not to see
That blanket of deceit
Which covered this hungry dog of the sea.
They all cry as they fall to the depth of the sea.

Folu Akintola (11)
St Saviour's and St Olave's School

A POEM IN MY POCKET

I've a poem in my pocket
And another in my head;
They come and go sometimes,
When I'm lying in my bed.

I waken in the morning
With a thought as new as day;
by the time I've had my cornflakes,
It's faded quite away.

Judy Antwi-Ohenewah (13)
St Saviour's and St Olave's School

LAST NOVEMBER!

Close my eyes, what do I see?
Layers of darkness in front of me.
I see something, it makes me think,
Is it a dream, or an intoxicating drink?
Swimming through water, miles wide,
Why am I here?
What's in my side?
As sharp as a knife, piercing me,
A pool of blood,
Forming in the sea.
Take a glance, a jagged piece of glass,
My side starts to sting, bleeding fast.
Overwhelming dizziness, a chill inside,
Floating up, I try to glide.
Starting to rise, my body's behind,
Feel the peace, no one can find.
Next thing I know, I hear ringing,
I think it's a dream, but my side is stinging.
Risk a look, I remember,
I bruised my side, last November!

Shamama Abulkhairi (13)
St Saviour's and St Olave's School

ALL ALONE

Never realised how lonely
All alone,
Friends no soul mates
No one cares,
Slipping away from everyone
No one to turn to,
No one to care for me
Everyone's got someone, not me
Different,
Not the same
I need him,
Not just any him
My him, no one else's
So alone,
No one understands
They've had someone
I haven't
All alone.

Clare Hillaby (14)
St Saviour's and St Olave's School

Woman-Child

I was a wayward child
with the weight of the world
that I held deep inside
life was a winding road
and I learnt many things
little ones shouldn't know.

But I closed my eyes
kept my feet on the ground
raised my head to the sky
and though times rolled by
still I felt like that child
as I look at the moon maybe
I grew up a little too soon

Nearing the edge I almost
fell right over
A part of me will never be able
to feel quite stable
that woman-child was on the verge
of fading inside
thankfully I woke up in time.

Carmen Gowie (11)
St Saviour's and St Olave's School

JUNK FOOD

Double chocolate gateau, chocolate chip muffin,
The traditional taste of a home-made stuffin'.
Cookies and cream, a '*Pizza Hut* supreme',
Twenty different flavours, in the ice-cream machine.
Mint chocolate chip, strawberry and banana:
Chocolate, and lemon with vanilla and sultana.
Burgers, beans and pie, with fries on the side,
Who cares about the diet rules, when food is on your mind?
Biscuit, crisps and sweets,
Were made for you to eat,
Don't force yourself to eat those foods containing fruit 'n' wheat.
Melted marshmallow, apple pie, icing on a cake,
Sausage in batter and a cheese potato bake.
Custard with apple strudel,
Chicken and mushroom noodles.
Pink, yellow candyfloss,
Big, round lollipops.
Fizzy, sticky orangeade, Pepsi Max, Lucozade
Oh just think if you could eat,
All this food within a week
How your stomach would go pop,
Before you try to cry out *stop!*

Bianca Jacobs (14)
St Saviour's and St Olave's School

The Dismor Waves Of The Sea

Whooshing calmly
through my ears
dripping drops drip
what I hear
warm sand
washed away by iced sea
cosy breeze rush
through my hair
storm disaster
comes to me
grey, blue blankets
cover the sea

Wherever I go
there's greyness ahead
silent at last
time to rest
blackness appears
diamond twinkling
over my head
the coolness
relaxing my mind
whoosh, whoosh . . .

Salina Ton (12)
St Saviour's and St Olave's School

CREATIVE CREATION

God created you and I
The same way he created the birds to fly,
He made the trees with leaves,
And some with honey for the bees.

This leaf that was given to me,
Has more meaning than I can see,
It has no pores but, yet it breathes,
It has no glands but it excretes.

The leaf has a spine that is clearly defined,
With evenly spaced thin short lines,
Although it appears not to be much,
All is revealed in just one touch.

Krystal Stewart (12)
St Saviour's and St Olave's School

WHAT BRINGS ME JOY?

What brings me joy?
The energy from the sun shining,
The rays which are sent down to make people smile.
A child's hug which brings warmth and comfort.
To bring a smile to a person's face,
When the wind catches my breath it fills me with
new life and vitality.
The moon, stars and sky which calms me when I am angry,
Which brings me comfort when I am hurt.
They relax my body, mind and soul, peace and tranquillity.
The word joy just says it all.
     Joy!

Chloe Trezel (12)
St Saviour's and St Olave's School

Shining Stars

Carry on twinkling little star.
There you are up above the sky.
You shine so bright and sparkle
like a diamond.
You make everyone's wishes come true.

Here I am looking above, wishing
on a star
I see the ocean of clouds which
spread around the world with the stars.

So as I sit here in the lonely field,
I gaze above at this amazing sky
and wish on my star for the
rest of my life.

Mumtaz Sadique (11)
St Saviour's and St Olave's School

Violent Night

Ship wrecking
Water wracking
Waves crashing
Sea monsters
Sea shells tumbling round
Wind whistling
Leaping waves
Howling waves
That is all I hear at night.

Farishta Karwani (12)
St Saviour's and St Olave's School

THE WINGS OF A DOVE

Sprouted from the seeds of harmony
An elegant bird
Whose lustrous snowflake complexion
Glows and turns gold
When the sun's rays stroke its feathers
What lies on the wings of a dove?
Not merely a cluster of feathers

It dances through the skies
Gliding gracefully
Its sleek white body cuts through the breeze
Like a blade
Clasping its angelic wings
It rises high into the air
A symbol of hope and prosperity
An icon of peace
Oh what lies on the wings of a dove?
Does the pressure of the countless evils in the world
Ever dishearten our feathered friend?

Guns are the loins of animosity
Enmity is the mother of evil
Hatred is the cause of war
War is the birth of death
This divine bird
Constantly combats against these concepts
Oh what lies on the wings of a dove!

Juliana Mensah (15)
St Saviour's and St Olave's School

WHISPERS OF DEATH

The sky is dark
the clouds are grey,
a storm is coming
coming our way.

I hear sounds far below.
The crashing tides deep but not low.

The moon hides,
from thee.
The whispers of death
cry out to me!

The murky, rough sea hits the shore,
turns around and comes back for more.

Raindrops drop from the sky
and hit the rocky ground,
the rhythmic beats start by and by,
that is where death will be found!

Slowly the storm becomes calm
and the moon comes out from hiding.
The grey clouds become clear
and the wind begins howling.

Slowly everything becomes quiet
the tides are calm and low.
The air was cold, the surface wet
all you could hear was death moan.

Sunna Komal Pervaiz (12)
St Saviour's and St Olave's School

SUN AND MOON

As the moon shines above at night
The sun comes up with all his might
But the moon, she will not go away
And the sun he wants to come and stay.

The battle of the night began
With Sparky the star as the referee man
A hit to the left and a hit to the right
As the sun he puts up a very good fight.

The moon is showing signs of weakness
But the sun he's being very merciless
'Will the battle ever end?'
Says Sparky who's going round the bend.

The moon has got a very big frown
Oh look at that she's fallen down!
And so I guess the sun is proud
'Congratulations' shout the crowd.

The battle of the night is done
It's over now, the sun has won!

Sharon Oteng (12)
St Saviour's and St Olave's School

WINTER

Just before winter the trees show their true colours
  Chestnut, brown, yellow and gold
The world is brighter without winter
  But then winter's claws take over the land
Turning it white, as white as a swan
  Winter has taken over the land
While animals are cosy and safe in their houses,
  Humans wander the Earth going to their various jobs,
They huddle together to keep away from winter's claws
  Animals patiently wait for the first day of spring,
But humans moan and complain
  Winter devours every sign of life and colour
Everything is dead or in hiding
  But soon spring will come and the land will brighten up
Animals and children will play together in harmony
  Plants will spring to life
The land will be green and lush, full of life
  I'll be waiting for that day
The day where I shall be free from the imprisoning winter
  But this is only a dream
But soon my dream shall be fulfilled.

Cherish Akinleye (11)
St Saviour's and St Olave's School

The Sun

The sun's light spreads across the land,
As it emerges like a yellow and orange fan.
Even as I stand here and the cold, salty wind blows,
The sun's piercing, warm rays oh so through me it flows,
Forever awakening me.

When summer is spent outside,
Here I look up as I lie,
And see a hot glowing yellow ball,
Its golden, bright splendour oh so on me it falls.
Spreading a sign of happiness on my face.

Where were you at sunset, the sunset soundlessly creeping away?
Like a disappearing mountain of gold under the pastel
multi-coloured array.
As I sit here watching you fade away as the day ends,
Your light gently touches me oh so through my heart it is sent,
Taking me back to the days when I was so young.

My life and light will vanish soon,
I am too fragile now and the children see me as a prune,
But I know what I will watch while I have my last breath,
The sun.
For it was always there and it shall, oh so till my sweet death.

Anna Friewald (15)
St Saviour's and St Olave's School

CREATION POEM

As a baby I was chubby and small,
With a frizzy hairstyle carved by a fall.
I was fed by my mum,
And dressed by my dad
And said a few words which made them glad.

But now I am older and ten foot tall
I get money off my dad and mum,
And smile and smile just like a sun.
I am rude to them which I think fine.
But to them they've wasted their time.

When I am older and more mature
I will straighten my hair after finding a cure
I will earn money after finding a job
And raise my children,
While suffering a lot.

Laura Johnson (12)
St Saviour's and St Olave's School

STORM POEM

In the storm,
Crashing waves,
In the storm,
Lots of rain,
In the storm,
Our boat is rocking,
In the storm . . .
. . . *Aarhh* look at that massive wave!

Natalie Jerrom (12)
St Saviour's and St Olave's School

THE VIEW

As I look out my window and stare,
I glare at the world so bare,
I notice the wind brush through the trees,
And the early risers go by as if bees,
And then suddenly a halt,
The clouds start to twitch,
A bright light and then I realise, the sun is coming out.

I'm in a dream, oh no, I wake up,
The sun has gone behind the woolly clouds,
And there's darkness to be found,
Droplets of water trickle down the window and blur the view.

The sun is back at last,
Peeping through the grey clouds,
I notice the chimney tops stretching far and wide,
The rooftops glinting with the fresh new light.

Colours dazzle me as I strain my eyes to see a beautiful rainbow,
Minutes roll by and the world gets dark,
I realise it is neither day nor night,
Mother's calling me, it's time for tea,
Oh, well the view will still be there tomorrow.

Filiz Altinoluk (11)
St Saviour's and St Olave's School

PEACE AND WAR

War the root of all evil, hatred death and above all conflict.
War can last days, weeks and often years bearing
grudges having no fears.
People enter war not knowing if they will come out alive
or dead, but at the time all you can see is red.

War only encourages more countries to compete where
hopefully they will complete their goal and win over the world.

After all the strain and the pain relief arises and peace is
begun until the silence is broken.

Victoria Hayden (16)
St Saviour's and St Olave's School

SUNSET

As I walk along the shore
I feel like I am a seagull.
A worn out seagull, that flew all
over the world and is now limping.
I look at the sunset, it is like
an orange sinking into a huge bowl of water.
But what if the sun was really an orange
and the sea was a huge bowl of water?
What if the sky was a chalkboard covered
with sky blue chalk?
Who knows? Do You?

Sufia Khatun (11)
St Saviour's and St Olave's School

FRIENDS

Friends are people who care
Friends are not to be used
Look after your friends
Friends are not to be left out
Try to understand your friends' feelings.

Friends are treated with respect
Friends are not judged by their looks
It's the inside that counts
So easy making friends
But not when it comes to keeping a friend.

Respect is the key word to keeping a friend
Trust your friends and they'll trust you
Never leave your friends out
Or take advantage of them
Or you end up with none.

Love your friends like you would
Love your family
Give all you can to care for your friends
Your friends don't just have you,
They have others, so never feel left out.

Arguing never works in friendship
If not your friendship is like a boat
Sinking down, down and never can get up,
Just like you
Losing your temper and hard to control.

Jackie Lai (13)
St Saviour's and St Olave's School

DECAYED TIME

When my time has ended, sweet love.
When life's clock has stopped,
And you can no longer understand the time,
Shall time's best jewel, from time's best chest, stay hidden?
Onward shall you go, out into the world,
Alone in person, my spirit in your heart.
Do not grieve for me, but take me in life's stride
And forget me not.
Tell many of my person, and the love that we shared.
Tell of our laughter and good times,
Remember not the bad.

And remember, dearest love,
Time may not choose one's death,
So live life as one should.

Leyla Guler (16)
Streatham High School

THE CHILDREN'S FAVOURITE SEASON

Autumn is a fun time of year,
Having leaf fights with all your friends.
Listening to the crisp and crunchy sounds of
The leaves as little children run through the huge piles.
People collect conkers which have fallen
from the tall frail chestnut trees,
So do the little squirrels before they hibernate.
the chilly and cold air gets quite windy.
Sometimes I like to walk against the breeze
to feel the wind through my hair.
I really enjoy autumn!

Olivia Firmin (11)
Ursuline High School

AUTUMN SCENES

Leaves a-crunching through the air,
Red and golden everywhere;
Falling gently like snowflakes white,
Through the day and through the night.

Conkers from oak trees, shiny, brown,
Their spiky shells on the freezing ground;
Berries on holly, poisonous, red,
Squirrels hibernating, underfed.

Pinecones, spiky, rough and brown,
An old barn owl embedded in its down;
Acorns with their little cups,
Flying south for the winter, are the ducks.

And as I walk through this beautiful scene,
Leaves a-rustling under my feet;
I look at the world, cold and dying,
The rain, drizzling, onto my head.

I think of home, a nice warm fire,
My pace is quickened, my spirits go higher;
I'm home now, in my nice warm bed,
Good night world, see you next spring!

Natalie Isaia (11)
Ursuline High School

AUTUMN IS HERE

Beautiful colours
Yellow brown
Falling lightly
Red green
Floating
Summer closes its eyes
Autumn is here.

I love the way the sun glistens
In the frosty morning
Close to freezing,
Come to warm
Many days to come
With chills and happiness.

Sian Wilson (11)
Ursuline High School

AUTUMN SORROW

The trees are desolate and dying,
The carpet of leaves are crying,
The sky is like a car exhaust all dark,
Polluted and cloudy.
The wind is very strong,
And bits of dust all flying,
The leaves are all beautiful,
But wrinkled and dying.
The colours are amazing,
They're brown, yellow and red.
The leaves are making something,
Which I'd call a leafy bed,
The wind is still dancing,
And drops are beginning to fall,
You can hear the crunchy leaves,
And the light rain falls.
Drops of rain following me,
I'm heading to my house,
Where it's nice, warm and cuddly,
And I can curl up like a mouse.

Holly Hawthorn (11)
Ursuline High School

Myself

This is a story about myself,
My name is Saba and I am twelve,
I used to live a long way away,
But now to England I've come to stay.
I have two brothers and sisters three,
We are a very large family.
I have black hair and dark brown eyes.
I'm not very tall but medium size.
I like to read and I like to write,
I like to draw pictures and colour them bright.
I do all my work and try to be good,
I respect all my teachers just as I should.
I love my family, and all my friends
And that's how my story finally ends.

Saba Hayat (12)
Ursuline High School

Autumn Ingredients

Autumn is here,
See the running deer,
Twigs and conkers,
Add some jumpers!
Leaves go orange, leaves go gold,
It's just too cold!
Red leaves, green leaves, brown ones too,
Add another spoon or two,
Hats and scarves, coats and boots,
Add some more autumn suits!

Hayley King (11)
Ursuline High School

My Possessions

The shoes that I got from day one,
Worn in the rain and in the sun.,
Given by my auntie, they smelt of sweet heather
They were made in Italy, from white patent leather.

When I was four, they just about fit,
At the new school they would be a hit.
My feet got bigger, so the shoes were replaced,
A cardboard box was where my old shoes were place.

Now I am eleven, they're still in that box,
Along with bits and pieces, like old glasses and socks.
I've had those shoes when I was really young
The white leather shoes I got from day one.

Athena Stavrakis (11)
Ursuline High School

Poem Of My Name

Q uetzal is my name I live in Stockwell Lane.
   I love going swimming and going
U nder water. I go to school on Mondays to Fridays and
   then in the
E vening I watch cartoons. It's fun.
T omorrow's another day to go to school and work, and
   sometimes I think of
Z ombies coming to get me, and
   taking me far
A way they take me to a place but I don't know
   where, they take me home in a
L ong and big spaceship.

Quetzal Rivas (11)
Ursuline High School

FRIENDS SHOULD BE...

Friends should be loyal,
people you can trust.
Friends should be funny
that quality's a must.

Friends should listen
and talk to you.
And come to visit
when you've got the flu.

Friends should keep secrets,
not tell everyone.
They should be kind
and they should be fun.

Friends should be grateful
to have you as a friend,
but you must respect them
if you want to stay friends.

Niyla Javaid (13)
Ursuline High School

MY FRIENDS

I have a friend who laughs and has fun.
But I do have others, she's not the only one.
They all share and care and we have a good time.
But in the end we do fall out of line.
We can laugh, we can talk it's good to
have a friend.
We can trust, we can party the fun will never end.
To make a best friend take it easy, take it slow,
So take good care and you'll never feel low.

Rochelle Sheldrick (11)
Ursuline High School

THE SEASON OF BEAUTY

The leaves are falling through the air
It's dark, it's cold, oh I'm scared.
I am walking down our long, long street,
The leaves are crunching under my feet.

I've been collecting all day long
Conkers, leaves, it's all the fun.
Walking round collecting conkers,
Shiny red ones, even brown ones.

The berries are beautiful but they're deadly
They start off orange but then they're red.
The colours are lovely red, yellow and orange.
It's raining fast I must go in.

It's raining, it's dingy it's dark and dull
Life is good, good as can be.
It's morning, it's fresh as fresh as can be
Dew has set now it's all for me.

It's one of my favourite seasons it is!
It's nice and fresh with things to collect.
I dream of this in my warm bed,
So seasons of beauty run through my head.

Jenny Davies (11)
Ursuline High School

My Possessions

I have a little piece of cloth,
That sleeps with me at night.
And when I go to bed,
I cuddle it so tight.

It's very very messy,
But I like it that way.
And when I go to someone's house,
I bring it along to stay.

It used to be a blanket,
That lay upon my bed,
But it got too big for me to carry around,
So Mum cut it up instead.

Imogen Barraclough (12)
Ursuline High School

The Veggie Race

The green team is up next!
It's peas, sprouts, spinach and broccoli!
Over they go to the popping plate.
The spoon takes charge now,
And up they fly to the dangly wobbler!
Down they go to the slippery slide!
Bluuuugh Ooooops!
And out they go again
(What a nasty sight)!
And the winners are the chicken dippers!
But sadly the losers are the gross green team.

Cristina Araujo (11)
Ursuline High School

THE VAIN PRINCESS

There once was a princess who was very vain,
She looked in the mirror over and over again!

One day a witch came along,
Singing a very happy song.

The princess was annoyed
To hear such beautiful singing,
That she stuck her head,
Out the window and said:
'Shut up, I say!
You are ruining my day,
For me to comb my beautiful hair,
For me to look at my face so fair!'

The witch got redder, for every word,
Which we all know,
Will bring on a curse . . .

On the end of the Princess' nose,
For all to see,
Was a horrible spot,
That was yellowy-green!

Sadly for her,
No one knew of a cure . . .
So a nose with a spot
Became her permanent lot!

Claudia Brady (11)
Ursuline High School

FRIENDS

My good friends are always there,
Without them it's like living with no air!

They are the ones I can always trust,
They're comforting, thank them I must.

With no friends I'm nobody,
When they are here I feel special.

When I'm angry my friendship is lost and
Is hanging,
No, of course not! My friends would understand.

When they are away I miss them all!
If they are ill, on the phone I'd give them a call!

Friends are like angels,
They can solve a miracle!

My friends are helpful,
They are making my happiness grow tall!

Natalie Solgala-Kaz (11)
Ursuline High School

MY FRIEND IMOGEN

This friend I am going to tell you about,
Is loud and noisy and likes to shout.
Yet she's funny and annoying too,
Sometimes she doesn't know what to do.

I've known her all through my life,
And she's always been the same inside.
A funny, annoying person,
Who can't always take a joke.
She's a friend to me and her name is
Imogen Barraclough.

Rachel Shepherd (11)
Ursuline High School

CHRONIC

All Sarah does is shop,
Shop, shop, shop.
Her blonde weary hair
And her puppy dog eyes say
Shop, shop, shop.
We go into town,
And I suddenly frown
For she's off to Galliano's boutique.
And no matter the price
She would never miss a slice of shoes, silk or pearls.
For goodness sake
I'm starting to shake
I ought to take a break and eat a small cake.
But what do I see, her with a sixty dollar steak.
If it weren't so comical
It would be diabolical.
Am I sardonic
Or is she a shoppaholic.

Gail Clark (13)
Ursuline High School

THE GULF WAR

Gather together blood and sand,
Use creaming method, mix by hand,
Place in a pan the water and oil,
And then very carefully bring to the boil.
Whisk in the chemicals and more blood,
And then maybe for flavour throw in a scud.
Mash up the missiles,
Garnish with pain,
Be careful, the blood tends to stain.
Grate up the corpses
Let the sun make them fry
And pick some young pilots
Fresh from the sky.
Chop up the pointlessness,
Blend in the hate,
Bake in the desert sun,
Serve on a place.
And just for decoration
On the top pour,
Hussain, the man who started this terrible war.

Nicola Burden (13)
Ursuline High School

MY FRIEND

She's my true mate,
She's not a person I would hate.
Always keeps my secrets inside,
And sticks by my side.

We may not often see each other,
But keep in contact with one another.
Our friendship will always be true,
We'd never want to start anew.

Rebecca O'Connor (11)
Ursuline High School

LOVE IS A BIRD

Love is a gift, which is often misunderstood.
Some people use it not as they should.

People take it upon them to welcome love in,
but the way it is thrown away
is cast as a sin.

If love took the place of injustice and pain,
perhaps we could learn and fairness we'd gain.

We wish there were no wars
no suffering or fright,
we often take for granted
we had a bed to sleep in at night.

Love is a mystery not to be found,
but all of our thoughts still circle
round and round.

In the end we can't understand it,
but we can always try,
for love is the bird that needs to fly.

Tanya Mehmet (13)
Ursuline High School

THE POLAR BEAR

The mighty polar bear prowls around the icy surroundings,
Looking over its frozen kingdom.
Its snowy coat camouflaged in the whiteness.
This impressive creature moves slowly,
Stalking its prey.
It sees the Arctic sun glow faintly,
Then cautiously dives into the bitterly cold water.
The polar bear swims powerfully towards the deserted seal.
And pounces.
It uses its strong neck to drag its victim over the pack ice.
After its meal the creature wanders off again
Towards its frozen realm.

Katie Jodoin (11)
Ursuline High School

MY POSSESSION

I have a little patchwork bag,
It's really something to brag about.

It's really colourful you see.
It isn't big, it isn't small,
Just in the middle.
It's not good to fiddle.

I hold it tight,
When I turn out the light,
And put it away at night.

I love my patchwork bag.

Monica Carvalho (11)
Ursuline High School

RACISM

Racism is evil
Racism is sin
Why is it allowed?
It shouldn't be let in.
People shouting names
As we walk down the street.
We're all the same really,
Colour's only skin deep.

No one should be treated
In such an awful way
People should be equals and that's how it should stay
Why do people think
They have the right?
To be so nasty and start all these fights

Racism is bad
Racism is wrong
Why do we judge so quickly?
It's gone on for too long.
Racism is nasty
Racism is cruel
If you are racist then you are a fool

Why do people do such awful, awful things
Why are people prejudiced against normal human beings?
Do they stop to think how much pain they're causing
In the future how will things have changed?
Will all colours walk the streets together?
Will they ever be the same?
Will they ever, ever change?

Ella Horswell (13)
Ursuline High School

WORLD WITH NO MACHINES

Imagine entering a new world,
A world with no machines,
No ovens to bake,
Or computers to make.
How would you live?

You would wash your clothes
In a well or stream,
You'd be working all day
With no rest or play.
How would you cope?

Imagine entering a new world,
A world with no machines.
No watches or clocks,
You'd be tied up in knots.
How would you tell the time?

Imagine entering a new world,
A world with no machines,
You would easily live,
You would easily cope,
Nobody needs machines!

Catriona Maria McCarthy (13)
Ursuline High School

SOMEWHERE FAR AWAY...

Somewhere far away,
The sun stays up all day
And goes to sleep at night.
When you wake up again,
You see, it shining bright.

It will be after us,
Because it's law of nature.
It will be after world,
That nobody could change . . .
Except the God.

Darya Syrpis (12)
Ursuline High School

OH, JUST LOOK AT THAT POOR FRAIL TREE

Oh, just look at that poor frail tree
Looking like it's hoping to be free.
Its poor dead branches with its poor dead leaves
I wish I could help it to be strong
Healthy with bright green leaves.
Oh, just look at that poor frail tree.

Oh, just feel the freezing wind,
Chilly with a sharp, dead touch.
Blowing its hardest bites at us.
Walking against the powerful breath
Everyone with a red nose and white face.
Oh, just feel the freezing wind.

Oh, just look at those bright colours
Golden and very attractive
Orange, brown, red and yellow.
Every shade you an imagine
Autumn has them all, all the thrilling colours
Oh, just look at those bright colours.

Virginia Stonehill (11)
Ursuline High School

MY HATES AND LIKES

They slither on walls,
They make slime everywhere,
Slugs.
I hate those things.

It's a type of vegetable,
covered in green.
Brussels sprouts.
I really hate that stuff.

They fly around although it's hard to see.
They are red with black spots.
Ladybirds
I like those things.

It looks like long worms,
But really they are long pieces of pasta.
Spaghetti
I love that stuff.

Pedrina Rodrigues (11)
Ursuline High School

HALLOWE'EN

Hallowe'en is dark like a witch's cat
Creepy people come like a bat
They say 'Trick or treat or smell my feet'
Whichever you pick, it will be real neat.

Kayenaat Gova (12)
Ursuline High School

Autumn Wonders

Dry leave crackle on the ground,
They remind me of fire, warm and burning,
I think of home, cosy and peaceful,
I start to run but slip on a conker,
Hard and shiny in a prickly shell.

The yellow sun glistens in the sky,
Although it's pale it places a warm glow in my heart;
I look around me at the wonders of autumn.
At last I arrive home,
And I look out of the window staring at the
Wonders of autumn.

Medena Knespl (11)
Ursuline High School

Autumn Has Arrived

Autumn is coming
trees are bare
it starts getting chilly in the air
you will find red and green leaves
shrivelled up ones too
the trees look dull and lonely
they only have one or two leave left
the air gets foggy and cold
the freezing winds start to come
animals like hedgehogs and squirrels
all start to hibernate
trying to bear the wind.

Delisa Ribaudo (12)
Ursuline High School

My Dream Of The World

My dream is for this world
to be a better place
for no more diseases or wars
for the poor to be off the streets
and in warm homes.

My dream for the world
is about hope and love
friendship and caring
joy freedom and happiness
for people to be united as one
as families and friends.

My dream for the world is
about the third world
I hope they have clothes
I wish they have food
to be loved and cared for.

Helen Onafowokan (11)
Ursuline High School

Autumn

The golden colours, cascade from the trees,
The powerful crunch from the fallen leaves.
The musky smell of the damp dew grass,
The warm sights of autumn make the year last.

The squirrels can prance from tree to tree,
The children will play gleefully.
The musky smell of the damp dew grass,
The warm sights of autumn make the year last.

Alice Marcar (12)
Ursuline High School

THE HEPHELUMP

I've had the hephelump,
That sits in the corner,
For years and years and years.

It had white whiskers,
But now they're grey,
'Cause I dragged him round all day.

Though I'm not the type to keep,
A pink teddy bear,
I've kept it for all these
Years and years and years.

And I'll keep it all year,
And I'll keep it all century,
And even a millennium,
But it will still smile in the corner
For all those years and years.

Maria Garbutt-Lucero (12)
Ursuline High School

Unhappy Autumn

The sleepy owl sits in its distant sleep.
As the old, tired and unhappy
willow tree shakes its crispy,
crunchy leaves to the ground.

As they drift sadly,
slowly to the ground,
as the bare tree watches
its leaves dance slowly to the ground.

Bright colours of red, orange
and golds sit there waiting to be
crunched like a packet of crisps or a burning pan.
Oh unhappy autumn just comes and goes.

Nicole Charles (11)
Ursuline High School

Weather Poem

Weather changes every day
Sometimes sunshine
Sometimes rain
Sometimes snow, sometimes frost
When there's fog you better not get lost

Lightning flashing in the sky
Thunder crashing close by

Snow for playing
Sun for bathing
The problem is the rain.

Reem Nasser (12)
Ursuline High School

Autumn Is Out There

Autumn is out there, bringing a cold snap,
There's a red and beigey brown carpet,
Scattered round a bare, frail tree.
I see someone out there,
Running from the wind,
As they run I hear
Spitting oil, burning paper, a crunch like crisp.
It looks like new life for the conkers
Which looked as if they were surrounded by soft creamy milk
Pine cones look spiky like a hedgehog.
Berries are bright red.
Not many acorns can be seen, as the squirrels have
Made a cold storage.

Joanna Foster (11)
Ursuline High School

My Teddy Bear

I have a bear, a teddy bear since I was four.
I have grown a lot since then and
I love it much more.
It's fell in dirt and slime and its arms and legs
were off when I was nine.
It's been many times sown together
and I will never give it away, *never!*
He's gone to different places and
seen so many faces.
I'll always keep to 'til I'm very old and
never leave it somewhere damp and cold.
When I am in trouble I will always give
this old bear a cuddle.
I love it do and I know it loves me too.

Karen Dempster (11)
Ursuline High School

AUTUMN POEM

The sun has gone miserable
The rain is coming down like cats and dogs.
The trees are getting cold as the leaves are falling
Brown ones, red ones, yellow ones, pinky ones.
It sometimes is like summer,
But not often.
The freezing winds,
The cold,
The darkness
And the dullness,
Are always around.
Nature is dying.
The children are crying.
The conkers are falling in and out of their shells.
The children are praying for snow and
The Lord will make sure we all have a fun and cold winter.
As well as safe.

Charlene Cumming (11)
Ursuline High School

MY POSSESSIONS

When I was about three years old
I got Miss Teddy, one of my favourite toys
She looked at me
When I went to bed
When I looked at her
I couldn't be upset

And now, I would never leave her
Because she is my friend.

Maria Kadziola (11)
Ursuline High School

My Hates And Likes

It's yellow and black
Its tail is long and sharp
As a pointed needle.
I really hate buzzing bumble beezzz.

It's green, it tastes delicious.
Gobble it up as fast as you can.
I really like green lettuce.

It's black, it has eight disgusting legs.
It's furry and spiky.
Yes! You've guessed it!
It's a s...p...i...d...e...r...

Liezl Ann Ornzo (11)
Ursuline High School

My Best Friend

My best friend is Monica,
Our friendship is unique.
We stick together all the time,
And we'll never be weak.

She's always in for a joke and a laugh,
And we have a joke, not half.
We see each other every day,
And we still have something good to say!

Even when we're old and grey,
Our friendship will never ever stray.

Izabela Stacewicz (12)
Ursuline High School

THE CHASE

Which way was the quickest?
I had to get there fast.
The man was still behind me.
Would I get home safe at last?

I crossed the road and ran.
It was getting pretty dark.
I dashed in-between cars on the road
and ran straight into the park.

He was *still* behind me!
I was getting really scared.
I couldn't see who it was,
however hard I stared.

My house was getting nearer,
but the fear was getting worse.
Then he shouted, 'Wait there don't move!
On the bus you left your purse!'

I ran to go and thank him.
Then he hit me with a brick.
It was only then I realised
It had only been a trick.

Laura Attipoe (13)
Ursuline High School

Autumn Has Come

Crackling crispy leaves, as you tread.
Beautiful colours, dropping off trees.
The wind is cold and bitter.
Howling round the dying lonely trees.
The sun a flickering dull colour,
It's getting darker by the second.
A puddle of water, a slippery hill.
Piles of dead and brightly coloured leaves.

A gusty wind a cold darting squirrel,
Collecting conkers.
A misty sky a driving rain.
A fast and furious wind howling like a scared dog.
Dewy grass covered with leaves,
That makes a squelching noise as you walk.
Dead twigs lie on the path.

A foggy night as I walked home.
A disliked wind a furious rain.
A whispering wind, a cloudy sky cold and gusty.
A lively rain flowing and dripping off trees onto my head.

It's a cold windy night and I wish I was indoors.
Snug in the warmth.
Instead I am out in the cold whispering, howling wind.
I am out in the flowing rain, and a dark sky.
At last I can see my home looming ahead.
At last I am inside in the warm and going to bed.

Charlotte Sewell (11)
Ursuline High School

LIAM BELL

His name was Liam Bell
He didn't like his school
When his sister came home
She found him in the hall.

Liam was bullied at school
By older boys than he
They said 'Give us taxes
Or you won't have your tea.'

He and his father
Started to really shout
What they never realised
Was the sadness that turned out.

Liam stormed upstairs
Where he found a tie
He was very shaken up
So he thought he'd jump and die.

Sadly his sister found him
Hanging from the stair
When she noticed it was Liam
She screamed with a scare.

So think everybody
What this did to him
Next time you go to church
Sing a little hymn.

Amy Allen (13)
Ursuline High School

Foxy Night

I look out my window,
and what do I see,
I see a small fox,
staring at me.

Its face is hidden,
but I look in its eyes,
it looks like it's trying
to put on a disguise.

The fox runs away,
into the night,
I can't see it anymore,
it has gone out of sight.

Emma Bye (13)
Ursuline High School

The Monster In My Closet

There's a monster in my closet
Crouching not to be seen
But waiting for the right time
You know, he's very keen.

He comes out in the dead of night
Roaming around and round
He's curious but cautious
Staying very low to the ground.

When the time has come I'll catch him
I know I will some day.
I'll train him to do many tricks
And teach him how to play.

Dahye Chung (13)
Ursuline High School

AUTUMN POEM

Leaves flowing everywhere,
In the cold windy air,
Rustling, rustic, crunchy legs,
Cold windy autumn breeze,
Cupped and curved,
Terracotta, fiery, golden, canary and butter.

Soggy, crumpled, crispy leaves,
Dancing and prancing in the breeze.
Pine cones - with a silvery shimmer,
Looks like they've got a lot of glitter.
Conkers, smooth, bumpy and rattling tapping on the ground.

Berries red, round and smooth, like mini cherry tomatoes.
Autumn is a season alone,
Which makes things change in
One whoosh of the wind.

Lehanna Young (11)
Ursuline High School

MY DREAM OF A NEW WORLD

My dream of a new world
Is very special to me
I dream that disease was never made
So people could live longer and feel no pain
Believe and fight for their human right
To love and see the world God had made
To learn and acknowledge how this world began
So let us all thank the Father, the Holy Spirit for
What they have done.

Antoinette Bynoe (12)
Ursuline High School

THE LIFE OF A LEAF

When I was young I was green and fresh,
Now I'm old and dull.
I've changed from young to old and weak,
Watch me change my colours as my energy leaks.
Pity me as I sit here dying,
Listen to the wind howling and crying.
Autumn's here and I'm filled with fear,
For the wind stands tall,
It's likely I'll fall.
Strong as a waterfall the rain will splish,
And I'll sit here wishing a wish,
That autumn will finish and I'll survive,
And I'll stay on this tree for the rest of my life.

Marianne Gray (11)
Ursuline High School

TELEPHONE SITUATION EVERY DAY

I was waiting in the line,
I wish there was a private telephone that was all mine.
I was waiting in the line like a fool,
I've just missed the third bus for school.

I really feel small against
These people, but I'm not I'm really tall.
But they keep pushing and shoving,
So I feel like I'm being bounced around like a ball.

I couldn't really see,
I think a telephone just went free.
But I couldn't get by,
So I decided to wait and sigh.

Natasha Gordon (12)
Ursuline High School

BULLIES' VICTORY!

They've won again,
They've destroyed a friend.
Nothing left,
But her breathing breath.
No spirit, no soul,
No life, no goal
Just a body with an empty hole.
But the battle goes on,
Like a tiring song.
When will they realise
What they're doing is wrong.
They've caused so much hurt
And so much pain,
Yet we're the ones who feel the shame.
Victims of a continuous crime
And I see no end to this needless rhyme.

Laura Bye (14)
Ursuline High School